HOW YOU CAN GET THE MOST
FROM THE NEW TAX LAW
**has one important purpose: to give you
a clear understanding of the new tax
law and its implications for your personal tax situation.**

The Economic Recovery Tax Act of 1981, signed
into law by President Reagan on August 13, 1981,
has been called the largest tax cut in history. It is
much more than that. Besides reducing income
tax rates by 23% over a three-year period, the new
law will help you in many other ways. It creates
and expands tax breaks already in the law—
which apply to individuals, corporations, trusts
and estates. Some people are saying the new law
affects only the rich and the super-rich. This is
not true. It applies to taxpayers in almost every
bracket. The time to take advantage of the new
tax law is now. This book is the place to start.

How You Can Get the Most from the New Tax Law

**Stuart A. Smith
and
Janet R. Spragens**

BANTAM BOOKS
TORONTO • NEW YORK • LONDON • SYDNEY

HOW YOU CAN GET THE MOST FROM THE NEW TAX LAW
A Bantam Book / October 1981

ISBN 0-553-20981-7

Published simultaneously in the United States and Canada

Bantam Books are published by Bantam Books, Inc. Its trademark,
consisting of the words "Bantam Books" and the portrayal of a
rooster, is Registered in U.S. Patent and Trademark Office and in
other countries. Marca Registrada. Bantam Books, Inc., 666 Fifth
Avenue, New York, New York 10103.

PRINTED IN THE UNITED STATES OF AMERICA

0 9 8 7 6 5 4 3 2 1

Contents

Part Three
Miscellaneous Provisions

List of Tables

Introduction

The Economic Recovery Tax Act of 1981, signed into law by President Reagan on August 13, 1981, has been called the largest tax cut in history. Over a three-year period, it will reduce income tax rates by 23 percent. But the reduction of tax rates is only one of the many ways the new law will help you. It also creates new tax breaks and expands many others already in the law that apply to individuals, corporations, trusts, and estates.

Some people are saying that the new law affects only the rich and the superrich. This is not true. The sweeping changes adopted by the new law, if properly taken advantage of, can provide planning opportunities and benefits for taxpayers in virtually every bracket. For this reason, it is important that you have a clear understanding of the new law and its implications for your personal tax situation.

How You Can Get the Most from the New Tax Law

attempts to give you that understanding so that you can make educated decisions that will save you taxes.

For example, you may have heard about the new tax-free savings certificates (called an "All-Savers Certificates") that the 1981 law created. These certificates can allow you (depending on your tax bracket) to earn tax-free interest at a rate roughly equivalent to a taxable interest rate of 20 percent. We'll show you here how to decide whether or not this is a good investment for you.

We also explain the new provisions for relief of the "marriage penalty," a quirk in the tax schedules that requires a two-income working couple to pay more income taxes than they would if they were single. We include planning tips about how to time your income and deductions to get the most from the new rate cuts, as well as information about a new law which allows you to deposit $2,000 each year in a savings account for your retirement and take a tax deduction for it.

In addition, we've attempted to explain, in simple English, the complicated new changes in the estate tax laws. There are easy planning techniques, like annual tax-free gifts to your children, that you can follow to reduce the estate tax bite at your death.

For many people, the new law has eliminated the estate tax altogether. Even if you are in this category, there are other considerations you should take into account in light of the new law, such as your current life insurance coverage.

If you own a business, you need to be aware of the dramatic changes in the depreciation rules, the investment credit, and the capital gains tax. If you have money to invest, you should know about the new maximum rate on the taxation of investment income, the new rules for excluding from your income part of the interest you earn each year, the new restrictions on "tax straddles" (a recently popular tax shelter technique), as well as the new All-Savers Certificates. To aid in understanding the new law, we've included strategy tips and the most commonly asked questions about the changes.

A lot of the provisions in the new law, to be sure, will automatically apply to you, without your having to do anything. In many cases, however, it is critical that you take some affirmative steps if you want to get the most out of the new law. Now is the time you should be making these planning decisions, not next year.

One caveat: this book cannot, of course, take the

place of a competent tax attorney if you are planning a major business or personal transaction or if you have a complicated tax problem and need specific legal advice. However, the information in this book can help you determine what information your lawyer may need and the right questions to ask. By becoming familiar with the new tax law, you'll save your lawyer time and save yourself legal fees.

By the way, *How To Get The Most from The New Tax Law* is tax deductible!

Stuart A. Smith and Janet R. Spragens

Washington, D.C.
October, 1981

Part One

Tax Changes for Individuals

1
Income Tax

Without question, the most heralded part of the new tax law is the income tax rate reductions over the next three years (1981–1984) on ordinary income and capital gains. Even if you sit back and do nothing, the tax rate cuts will leave you with more spendable income. But changes in the rates over the next three years create opportunities for you to save more tax dollars by careful timing of income and deductions. Let's see how it can be done.

Income Tax Rate Cuts

Prior to the 1981 law, everyone with a taxable income in excess of $3,400 on a joint return and $2,300 on a single return had to pay income tax. The rates at which you were charged began at 14 percent of your income and ranged up to 70 percent at progressive intervals. The progressive intervals make the income tax a "graduated" tax. As the tables in Appendix A show, this means that your first dollars of income are taxed at a lower rate than your last dollars of income. When someone says he is in the 40 percent bracket, it does not mean that all of his income is taxed at a 40 percent rate. It simply means that the last few thousand dollars are taxed at this rate. In this example, the 40 percent category is sometimes called the "marginal" rate. The highest rate (70 percent) applies to taxable income of $215,400 or more for joint returns and $108,300 or more for individual returns. Because the income tax is graduated, the higher your marginal rate, the greater your savings from deductions from income. For example, $1 of deduction is worth 14 cents to someone in the 14 percent bracket but 50 cents to someone in the 50 percent bracket. A credit, on the other hand, is a direct dollar offset against your final tax bill. If you have a positive tax liability, a $1 credit will therefore be more valuable than a $1 deduction.

The tax laws also set a maximum tax of 50 percent for "earned income" or "personal service income." Personal service income consists of income items like wages, salaries, commissions, professional fees, and royalties. You should note that this is different from "unearned income," which is made up of income from such "passive" sources as interest and dividends. Under the old law, unearned income could be taxed above the 50 percent rate, although earned income was subject to no more than a 50 percent tax rate.

The Economic Recovery Tax Act of 1981 provides enormous tax relief to you. First of all, it cuts taxes across the board by reducing the actual tax rates at which you are charged. These rate reductions are substantial and have been popularized as a three-year 25 percent cut, to take effect as follows: 5 percent in the first year, 10 percent in the second year, and 10 percent in the third year. Because these cuts were scheduled to take effect in October 1981 rather than at the first of the year, the reductions are phased in four stages as follows: 1.25 percent in 1981, 10 percent in 1982, 19 percent in 1983, and 23 percent in 1984 and thereafter. Included in these "across the board cuts" is a reduction in the overall rate from 11 percent to 50 percent rather than the prior law's 14 percent to 70 percent rates. Furthermore, the new law reduces the maximum tax rate on *all* income, earned and unearned, from whatever source, from 70 percent to 50 percent. This reduction is a major change, and as we see later, it can affect many of your tax-planning strategies. The 50 percent maximum rate becomes effective as of January 1, 1982.

What tax break should you expect for 1981?

The 1981 tax rate cut will be implemented by permitting you to take a 1.25 percent tax credit against your regular tax liability for the year, which is applied

3

before any other tax credits. For example, suppose you are a married taxpayer and that you and your spouse have taxable income for 1980 of $30,000. If you file a joint return, your tax bill for the year will be $6,238. For 1981-1984, if your taxable income remains the same, your taxes will be reduced as shown in Table 1:

Table 1
SAMPLE TAX REDUCTION UNDER THE NEW LAW

	1981	1982	1983	1984
Tax liability	$6,160.03	$5,607	$5,064	$4,818

Thus, your 1981 tax liability reflects the 1.25 percent credit implemented by the new law. For the entire period however, your tax bill under the new law will drop a total of $1,342.03.

How will the amount of tax taken out of your paycheck each week be affected?

In order to reflect these changes, income tax withholding rates (i.e., the schedule of rates your employer uses to withhold taxes from your paycheck) are scheduled to go down as follows:

- a 5 percent rate reduction effective October 1, 1981
- a 10 percent rate reduction effective July 1, 1982
- a 10 percent rate reduction effective July 1, 1983

Because the 1981 tax cut is effective for only part of the year as of October 1, your withholding taxes will go down only 1.25 percent for the period October 1 through December 31, 1981.

What about the capital gains tax?

The act also reduces, to 20 percent, the maximum tax rate on long-term capital gains for sales or exchanges of property like stocks or real estate, a change that has been made retroactively effective as of June 9, 1981.

4

Both before and after the new law, your tax on the sale of a capital asset will be computed permitting a 60 percent deduction of your gain from gross income. The result was and is that only 40 percent of the gain is subject to tax. Under the old law, however, the maximum tax rate was 70 percent; therefore, the maximum tax that could be applicable to a capital gain was 28 percent (40 percent × 70 percent). The 1981 act reduces the maximum rate to 50 percent. By doing so, it has automatically reduced the maximum rate on capital gains to 20 percent (40 percent × 50 percent). The general reduction in the maximum rate from 70 percent to 50 percent is not effective until January 1, 1982. By a special transitional rule, however, the 20 percent maximum rate on capital gains is made retroactively effective as of June 9, 1981. Without this special rule, the maximum capital gains tax would remain at 28 percent until January 1, 1982.

If you are above the 50 percent bracket and have long-term capital gains that you could realize before the end of the year, it doesn't matter whether you take them this year or in 1982. The maximum tax will be 20 percent under the special transitional rule. If your income puts you below the 50 percent bracket, you should try to postpone long-term capital gains until 1982 in order to take advantage of the lower tax rates.

Strategy Tip

To maximize your tax savings under the new act, where possible, you should try to shift as much of your income ahead, into the years when the full benefit of the tax reductions will take effect. By doing this, you will make this income taxed at a lower rate. Moreover, you will postpone the payment date for the taxes due on the income, thereby getting extra use of that money. For example, if you are self-employed, you may want to wait to send year-end bills out until January 1982, January 1983, or January 1984. In seeking to shift your income, however, you should be careful of situations in which the income might be treated as being part of your earnings (for tax purposes) currently even though you haven't physically received the money. The tax law doesn't permit you to avoid current tax on any income items that are subject to your unqualified demand or control, like interest that is credited to your savings account that you do not actually draw down before the end of the year, even though you haven't actually received the cash in hand.

Also, particularly if you are in a bracket above 50 percent in 1981, you should try to accelerate as many of your deductions as you can into 1981 because these deductions will have maximum impact in reducing your tax bill when the rates are higher. For example, if you prepay all of your 1981 state taxes in December 1981 instead of on April 15, 1982, when they are finally due, you can claim the amount as a deduction on your 1981 federal return. Early payment of professional or union dues, medical expenses, and/or business magazine and newspaper subscription costs may also provide you with more deductible expenses for the current year. Simply put, to the extent you can get your taxable income down when the rates are higher, the rate differential will save you dollars.

The benefits to be gained by shifting income into subsequent years when the rate cuts are deeper are dramatically illustrated in Table 2. It shows the effect of the rate reductions on single and married taxpayers, as well as the cuts in the marginal rates of everyone across the economic spectrum.

Indexing

Beginning in 1984, the new law requires the income tax code to be revised annually to avoid what is sometimes referred to as "bracket creep." Bracket creep may sound like a contagious disease, but in tax parlance it is a phenomenon that pushes you into a higher tax bracket through incremental wage increases that really only keep up with inflation. For

Table 2
THE EFFECT OF THE TAX CUT
SINGLE TAXPAYERS
TAX LIABILITY*

Taxable Income†	1980	1981	1982	1983	1984
$ 5,000	$ 442	$ 417	$ 368	$ 341	$ 325
10,000	1,387	1,370	1,233	1,121	1,075
15,000	2,605	2,572	2,330	2,097	2,001
20,000	4,177	4,125	3,752	3,369	3,205
25,000	5,952	5,878	5,362	4,829	4,565
30,000	7,962	7,862	7,172	6,477	6,113
40,000	12,657	12,498	11,408	10,313	9,749
50,000	18,067	17,841	16,318	14,738	13,889
75,000	33,393	32,976	28,818	26,973	25,571
100,000	50,053	49,427	41,318	39,473	37,935
150,000	84,887	83,826	66,318	64,473	82,935
200,000	119,887	118,388	91,318	89,473	87,935

* Ordinary income rates, without regard to the maximum tax on earned income.
† Gross income, less deductions and personal exemptions.

7

Table 2 (Continued)

MARRIED COUPLES FILING JOINT RETURNS
TAX LIABILITY*

Taxable Income†	1980	1981	1982	1983	1984
$ 5,000	$ 224	$ 221	$ 368	$ 176	$ 176
10,000	1,062	1,049	1,030	864	819
15,000	2,055	2,029	1,823	1,676	1,581
20,000	3,225	3,185	2,893	2,606	2,461
25,000	4,633	4,575	4,153	3,760	3,565
30,000	6,238	6,160	5,607	5,064	4,818
40,000	10,226	10,098	9,195	8,304	7,858
50,000	14,778	14,593	13,305	12,014	11,368
75,000	27,778	27,431	25,055	22,614	21,468
100,000	41,998	41,473	37,449	34,190	32,400
150,000	73,528	72,609	62,449	59,002	56,524
200,000	109,032	105,694	87,449	84,002	81,400

* Ordinary income rates, without regard to the maximum tax on earned income.
† Gross income, less deductions and personal exemptions.

Table 2 (Continued)
SINGLE TAXPAYERS
MARGINAL RATE (%)

Taxable Income†	1980	1981	1982	1983	1984
$ 5,000	18	18	16	15	14
10,000	21	21	19	17	16
15,000	30	30	27	24	23
20,000	34	34	31	28	26
25,000	39	39	35	32	30
30,000	44	44	40	36	34
40,000	49	49	44	40	38
50,000	55	55	50	45	42
75,000	63	63	50	50	48
100,000	68	68	50	50	50
150,000	70	70	50	50	50
200,000	70	70	50	50	50

† Gross income, less deductions and personal exemptions.

Table 2 (Continued)

MARRIED COUPLES FILING JOINT RETURNS
MARGINAL RATE (%)

Taxable Income†	1980	1981	1982	1983	1984
$ 5,000	14	14	12	11	11
10,000	18	18	16	15	14
15,000	21	21	19	17	16
20,000	24	24	22	19	18
25,000	32	32	29	26	25
30,000	37	37	33	30	28
40,000	43	43	39	35	33
50,000	49	49	44	40	38
75,000	54	54	49	44	42
100,000	59	59	50	48	45
150,000	64	64	50	50	50
200,000	68	68	50	50	50

† Gross income, less deductions and personal exemptions.

10

example, if you are single and earned $21,000 in 1980, you would be in the 34 percent bracket. If you received a $3,000 raise in 1981, you would automatically be pushed up and into the 39 percent bracket. Yet in real dollar value, your less-than-15-percent salary increase might barely keep up with inflation. Thus, in terms of inflation, the effect of the progressive tax rates has been to impose heavier tax burdens when you receive wage increases, but your "buying power" often remains in the same economic position.

When will the indexing adjustments occur?

Under the 1981 act, Congress has required an annual adjustment of the tax brackets to reflect increases in the cost of living as measured by the Department of Labor's Consumer Price Index (CPI). The adjustments are to be made no later than December 15 each year, effective for the following year. These adjustments are nothing short of revolutionary, for they represent a recognition by Congress that the government should not benefit from inflation through increased tax revenues.

What else will be indexed besides the tax brackets?

The new law also requires inflation indexing of the $1,000 you get automatically as a personal exemption and the minimum amount of income that is not subject to tax, sometimes called the "zero bracket amount."

The first adjustment will be made in 1984 (for 1985 tax purposes), and adjustments will then follow annually.

Estimated Income Taxes

There are two methods that the Internal Revenue Service (IRS) uses to collect income taxes. First, it requires employers to withhold taxes from their employees' wages. Second, it demands that if you earn "nonwage income," such as dividends, interest, and earnings from self-employment, you must file an estimated tax return four times a year (April 15, June 15, September 15, and January 15) and make accompanying estimated payments so that the taxes due are currently paid. Failure to do this can trigger a penalty.

Strategy Tip

In figuring out your estimated income tax for the remainder of 1981, don't forget to take into account the 1.25 percent reduction (5 percent × $^1/_4$) because of the October 1, 1981, effective date of the new law. If you've missed out on the September 15, 1981, payment, you can still subtract the tax cut from your January 15, 1982, payment.

Who has to file an estimated tax return?

Under the prior law, you were required to file quarterly estimated tax returns and make quarterly payments if you earned $100 or more during the year. The new law increases that $100 threshold amount to $500 over a five-year period (Table 3):

Table 3
WHAT YOU MUST EARN BEFORE AN ESTIMATED RETURN IS REQUIRED

Year	Threshold Amount
1981	$100
1982	200
1983	300
1984	400
1985 and thereafter	500

If your income is not subject to withholding by your employer and if you earn less than the threshold amount, then you do not have to file an estimated tax return or pay an estimated tax. Also, you won't be subject to any penalties for underpayment of your estimated tax.

Charitable Deductions for Nonitemizers

The tax law has long permitted a deduction from income for charitable contributions made during the year. A charitable contribution has always been considered to be a personal deduction rather than a business deduction. Thus, under the prior law, if your personal deductions as a whole amounted to less than the zero bracket amount, you could not itemize and therefore could not separately claim your charitable contributions as a deduction.

For a limited time, the new law now allows a portion of these charitable contributions to be claimed despite the fact that you do not separately itemize your personal deductions (Table 4).

However, the amount of the relief is small. For 1982 and 1983, 25 percent of your charitable contributions up to $100 of your contributions is deductible. You can claim a charitable deduction under the new provision, therefore, of up to $25. For 1984, the applicable percentage is still 25 percent, but it can apply against up to $300 of charitable contributions. The maximum deduction is therefore $75. For 1985, 50 percent of your charitable contributions up to $300 will be directly deductible, for a maximum deduction of $150. Finally, in 1986, 100 percent of up to $300 of your charitable

Table 4
CHARITABLE CONTRIBUTION
DEDUCTION FOR NONITEMIZERS

Year	Applicable (%)	Maximum Contributions	Maximum Deduction
1982	25	$100	$ 25
1983	25	100	25
1984	25	300	75
1985	50	300	150
1986	100	300	300

contributions is deductible, for a maximum deduction of $300.

That's the end of the line, however. After 1986, charitable contribution deductions are once again only available to itemizers, as under the prior law.

Of course, those of you who itemize are entitled throughout this period to claim all of your charitable deductions, as before.

2
The Family

The new tax law provides many new tax savings opportunities that relate to your family. The one that has been the most publicized is the provision that has allowed relief from the so-called marriage penalty. But there are other equally significant changes, and many of these could directly affect you.

Marriage Tax Penalty

For years, two-earner married couples have complained that the tax laws unfairly discriminate against them because they were subject to a higher combined income tax than two single people in a similar financial situation.

This problem is popularly known as the "marriage penalty." It derives not from a special tax on married couples but from a quirk in the tax rates that has resulted in different tax burdens being imposed on single and married taxpayers. Under the Economic Recovery Tax Act of 1981, there is some relief from the marriage penalty.

What exactly is the marriage penalty?

The following example shows how it works. Take the case of Joe and Ann O'Brien, a married couple whose taxable income in 1980 is $30,000. All of this money is earned by Joe. A look at the tax tables shows that they will pay a total tax of $6,238. By comparison, Susan Evans, a single individual with the same $30,000 icome, will pay $7,962 in tax! In this situation, being married, with the accompanying privilege of being able to file a joint return, has clearly worked a benefit to the married wage earner. It is the single taxpayer who is penalized because with the same $30,000 income, she pays $1,724 more in taxes.

If, however, we take another married couple, Tony and Mary Luciano, of whose $30,000 income each earns $15,000, and compare them with two single taxpayers, Jim Petry and Linda Wong, who earn $15,000 each, the problem begins to emerge. In this situation, the Lucianos' joint liability will still be $6,238, but under the tax tables the two single individuals, each with $15,000 of taxable income, have an individual tax liability of $2,605 (or a combined tax burden of $5,210). In these circumstances, then, it is the Lucianos who bear the greater tax burden. If the married couple were unmarried and simply living together, they would save $1,028. It is this "cost" of getting married that is commonly known as "the marriage penalty."

Why can't the rates be equal?

Prior to 1969, the rates applicable to single taxpayers were the same as those applicable to married taxpayers filing separately. Thus, two single taxpayers earning $10,000 each would pay tax at the same rate as a married couple where each spouse earned $10,000. However, this intensified the disparity in tax treatment between single and married taxpayers where one of the spouses earned *all* of the couple's income and the couple filed a joint return. This was, in fact, a "marriage benefit" or a "single's penalty." In some instances, the pre-1969 rates produced a "single's penalty" that resulted in a single person's tax being as much as 40 percent greater than the tax of a married taxpayer with the same income who filed a joint return.

In 1969, Congress decided to ease the tax burden of the single taxpayer. It reduced the singles' tax rates but left untouched the rates applicable to married taxpayers, whether they filed joint or separate returns.

The result was twofold. The filing of joint returns produced a "marriage benefit" in the case of the family in which one spouse earned most or all of the couple's

16

combined income. However, it also produced a "marriage penalty" as the couple's two paychecks become roughly equal.

What causes the "marriage penalty" or the "singles' penalty"?

Very simply, it is the convergence of three inconsistent goals of the tax laws: (1) that the rates be progressive so that as a person's income goes up, it is subject to a higher-percentage tax rate; (2) that married couples be able to file joint returns combining their income and deductions even though one spouse earns all the income and/or incurs all the deductible expenses; and (3) that equal-income taxpayers (whether single or married) bear equal tax burdens. If goals (1) and (2) are met, it is mathematically impossible to reach goal (3). Either the laws discriminate against single taxpayers (as they did prior to 1969 and partly today) or they discriminate against married taxpayers (as they do under the present rate structure in some cases).

How does the new law help two-earner married couples?

In order to give some relief to two-earner married taxpayers in this situation, short of scrapping the whole concept of the progressive rate structure and joint returns, the 1981 law provides a partial solution after 1981. Under the law, married couples are permitted a 10 percent deduction (except in 1982 when it allows only 5 percent) of the "qualified earned income" (defined below) of the spouse with the lesser amount of income up to a maximum of $30,000 of such income. Thus, the maximum deduction is $1,500 for 1982 and $3,000 for 1983 and thereafter. By basing the deduction on the "qualified earned income" of the spouse with the smaller income, the law relieves some of the burden of two-earner couples but doesn't enhance the

17

marriage benefit where there is only one breadwinner in the family. This deduction is available even if the couple doesn't itemize their deductions.

"Qualified earned income" is earned income from sources such as wages, commissions, or fees (as opposed to "passive sources" such as interest or dividends) minus all the business expenses attributable to earning this income and any contributions to IRA, Keogh, or other pension plans for the year. It also must be income that is subject to tax. Income from pension annuities, IRA distributions, and deferred compensation is specifically excluded from the definition of qualified earned income, as is salary income paid by one spouse to the other. Also excluded are unemployment compensation benefits. In addition, state community property laws are disregarded when computing the earned income of the spouse with the smaller income.

By limiting the deduction to earned income, the new law seeks to reduce the tax disincentive against the second spouse entering the work force. Also, couples claiming the benefits of the foreign income exclusions are barred from claiming the new marriage penalty relief.

Table 5 traces the effect of the new deduction in 1981, 1982, 1983, and 1984 on a married couple and an unmarried couple. Both couples have a total income of $60,000, half of which is earned by each partner. Assuming itemized deductions for each couple are the

Table 5
REDUCTION IN MARRIAGE PENALTY UNDER THE NEW LAW

	1981	1982	1983	1984
Married couple	$14,303	$12,381	$10,574	$10,000
Unmarried couple	11,986	10,934	9,850	9,310
Marriage penalty	2,317	1,447	724	690

same ($12,000), the taxes paid by them will be as shown in Table 5.

Table 5 shows the tax relief created under the new law for two-earner couples but also shows that the changes have not totally eradicated the marriage penalty.

Child- and Dependent-Care Credit

Those of you who want your children to be a credit to you are in better shape than you might think. Under legislation first enacted in 1976 and now liberalized by the 1981 law, a tax credit is available for expenses you incur for child and dependent care that permit you to be gainfully employed.

How is the credit different from prior law?

Under the prior law, a tax credit for child-care expenses was also allowed, but it was limited to a maximum of 20 percent of the expenses incurred, up to $2,000 for one child or $4,000 for two or more. The maximum credit that you could claim was therefore $400 for one child (20 percent × $2,000) or $800 for two or more children (20 percent × $4,000). The 1981 law, which becomes effective as of January 1, 1982, increases both the percentage of child-care expenses that you can claim as a credit *and* the maximum amount of total expenses to which you can apply the percentage.

If your income is $10,000 or less, the act now permits a maximum credit of for child-care expenses of 30 percent of a maximum of $2,400 for one child or 30 percent of a maximum of $4,800 for two or more children. Thus, the maximum credit for taxpayers earning $10,000 or less is now $720 for one child or $1,440 for two or more children, as opposed to $400 or $800 under the old provision.

For taxpayers earning between $10,000 and $28,000, the 30 percent credit is reduced one percentage point for each $2,000 (or fraction of $2,000) of income between $10,000 and $28,000. For example, if you earn between $10,000 and $12,000, the maximum credit is 29 percent of the expenses, for a maximum credit of $696 for one child or $1392 for two or more children. If you earn between $12,001 and $14,000, the maximum credit is 28 percent; and so forth.

However, the maximum amount of expenses to which these percentages can apply remains contant for all tax brackets, and the most you could ever deduct is $2,400 for one child and $4,800 for two or more children.

For taxpayers with annual incomes above $28,000, 20 percent of the child-care expenses (as under prior law) is still the most that can be claimed. But since the 20 percent is now applicable to $2,400 of allowable expenses for one child or $4,800 for two or more, even the taxpayers in these higher brackets will benefit from the increased credit. The maximum credit has been increased for one child from $400 to $480 (20 percent $\times$ $2,400) and for two or more children from $800 to $960 (20 percent $\times$ $4,800).

Do any rules carry over from the prior law?

Most of the same rules apply as under the old law. The child- and dependent-care expenses you incur are only eligible for credit to the extent they allow you to be gainfully employed. This means if you are single, your child-care costs can't be more than you earn for the year. If you are married, your credit cannot be more than the income of the spouse earning the lesser amount of the family income.

There is one exception, however, for cases in which one spouse is a full-time student or is incapable of caring for himself or herself. This exception has been expanded under the new law. In these cases, the student or the disabled spouse is deemed to have earned $200 per month (if the couple has one child) or $400 per month (if they have two or more children) for purposes of figuring the earned-income limitation.

This fictional income figure applies for each month the spouse fits into the category of being a full-time student or a disabled person. The $200 and $400 figures are an increase over the prior law in which $166 and $333 constituted the fictional monthly amounts allowed.

For example, assume Michael and Helen Goldman have an adjusted gross income of $34,000 in 1982, all of which is earned by Tom. Helen is a full-time law student for nine months out of the year and has no earned income. During the year, Michael and Helen incur $3,000 of expenses for household services and child care for their 3-year-old son. Under the earned-income limitation, without the special provision for full-time students, the couple could not claim a child-care credit because Helen didn't earn any income. Under this exception, however, Helen will be deemed to have $1,800 (9 × $200) of earned income for the year and will therefore be permitted to claim a child-care credit of $360 (20 percent of $1,800). If they had two children, the maximum credit would be $600 (20 percent of $3,000).

What expenses qualify for the new credit?

The new law also broadens the class of expenses that qualify for the credit. Under the prior law, you could deduct only your payments for services outside the home for a dependent under fifteen years of age and if the dependent was claimed as a personal exemption. Now a dependent of any age is eligible if the care is provided by a dependent-care center and the dependent spends at least eight hours a day in the taxpayer's home.

In addition, the new law also provides that where your employer furnishes day-care services to you without charge, the value of the services aren't considered part of your taxable income. Of course, if this happens, you haven't spent any money for the day-care benefits, and therefore you can't claim any child-care credit.

Strategy Tip

To be able to substantiate on audit the payment of your child- and dependent-care costs, you should pay all of these costs by check.

Also, the law permits payments to relatives (such as a grandmother) to qualify for the child-care credits as long as the relative is not a dependent whom you plan to claim as a personal exemption or a child of yours under the age of nineteen.

Child Adoption Expenses

Beginning in 1981, a new $1,500 deduction was created for adoption expenses of children "with special needs." Children with special needs are defined in the new law as children with respect to whom payments are made under the adoption assistance program of Section 473 of the Social Security Act. That program is for children who have been found by the state to be eligible for adoption assistance because there is a specific factor that leads the state to believe that these children cannot be placed without adoption assistance.

Social Security payments do not cover or reimburse the expenses, in connection with the adoption of a child, such as attorneys' fees and court costs. The payments are limited to ongoing maintenance payments of the child.

The new law now makes deductible what the Social Security law doesn't reimburse. However, the adoption expense provision specifically bars a deduction for any expenses paid through a federal, state, or local program. In addition, it specifically prohibits a deduction for any part of the adoption expenses that can be claimed under another provision of the tax law.

3
Real Estate

The 1981 tax law contains a number of changes specifically aimed at home owners. These changes provide important opportunities to ease the tax burdens on the sale of your personal residence and should be carefully reviewed if you're thinking about selling your home.

Once-in-a-Lifetime Exclusion

When the Revenue Act of 1978 was adopted, it added a provision to the Internal Revenue Code permitting taxpayers fifty-five years old or older to elect to completely exclude from their taxable incomes up to $100,000 of gain realized on the sale of a personal residence. Under the 1981 act, that amount has been increased to $125,000.

How does the provision work?

To qualify for the exclusion, you must be fifty-five years or older *before the sale* and must have owned and used the home as a personal residence for three years out of the five-year period immediately preceding the sale. The provision not only applies to sales of houses; it also covers condominium sales, and sales of stock in a co-op. If you're married, own your property jointly with your spouse, and file joint returns, only one of you has to meet the age, use, and holding period requirements.

To elect the exclusion, you should attach a signed statement to your tax return for the year in which you make the sale. The statement must indicate your intent to elect the exclusion and must also show the following:

- The cost of the residence at the date of purchase

- The date of the purchase
- The date of the sale
- The names and social security number of all of the owners of the residence as of the date of sale
- The form of ownership and the age and marital status of the owners at the time of sale
- The duration of any absences (other than vacations or other seasonal absence) by the owners during the five-year period preceding the sale
- Whether any of the owners has previously made an election under this provision, and if so, the details of such election.

If you only use part of the exclusion, can you "save" the rest for another sale?

No. You should note that once the exclusion has been claimed even in part, it cannot be claimed again. It is a one-time exclusion only. Therefore, even if you use less than the statutory amount, the balance cannot be "saved" and applied to another home sale.

In addition only one lifetime exclusion is allowed for a married couple. If you file separate returns, each of you may claim only one-half of the exclusion. If, subsequent to claiming the exclusion, you get a divorce, neither of you may claim another exclusion. Nor, if you remarry and jointly buy another home can your new spouses claim the exclusion.

Even if you can satisfy the ownership and use the requirements for only part of your residence (e.g., part of your residence is used as an office), you are still eligible to claim the exclusion, but only with respect to the part of the gain that applies to the residence portion of the property.

The increase in the exclusion to $125,000 applies to all sales made after July 20, 1981.

The "Rollover" Provision

The new law also extends, from eighteen months to two years, the "replacement period" within which you can sell a principal residence at a gain and then buy other property in order to avoid an immediate tax.

Since 1954, the law has permitted taxpayers who sell a personal residence at a profit to postpone taxation of the gain if the money received from the sale is "rolled over" and reinvested in another personal residence. If the new home costs more than the selling price of the old home, none of the gain will be recognized for tax purposes. If, on the other hand, the new home costs less than the sales price of the old home, deferral of the gain on the first home is still permitted, but only to the extent of the reinvestment in the new home. The difference will be subject to tax. In either case, the unrecognized profit is then subtracted from the cost of the new home for tax accounting purposes to determine the gain realized on that property at the time of its sale.

The following example shows how the provision works:

Suppose you decide to sell a residence you had bought for $100,000 in 1972. In August 1981, you sell the house for $275,000. Brokers' commissions and other selling expenses total $12,000. In October 1982, you buy a new residence for $300,000. Your gain and amount available for tax deferral are computed in Table 6:

Table 6
COMPUTATION OF ROLLOVER ON GAIN ON RESIDENCE SALE

Selling Price	$275,000
Less: commissions and other selling expenses	12,000
Amount realized on the sale	263,000
Less: cost of home	100,000
Amount realized	163,000
Cost of purchasing new home	300,000
Gain subject to tax	0
Gain deferred	$163,000

What happens when you sell the second residence?

When you sell the second residence, which you bought for $300,000, the amount of gain will be measured by the sale price less $137,000 (300,000 − 163,000). Thus, the gain that has been deferred from the sale of the first house will be taxed at that time.

Of course, if the gain on that house is then reinvested in a third, that gain can also be deferred if the requirements of the statute are met. Unlike the $125,000 lifetime exclusion, the rollover provision can be applied over and over again as you "trade upward" to larger or more expensive residences. One caveat: only one rollover is permitted per replacement period. There are special rules, however, for multiple-sale rollovers within a short time period if caused by a job-related move.

Strategy Tip

If you're contemplating a sale of a personal residence, you should carefully consider how the $125,000 exclusion and the rollover provision can be used together to maximize the tax savings potential of each. For example, if the gain on the sale of your house is more than $125,000 and you reinvest the proceeds in a more expensive residence, the law permits you to elect to exclude $125,000 of the gain and defer the balance under the rollover provision. Or you can defer the entire gain and utilize the one-time exclusion at some later date, such as when you sell your last residence and move to an in-town rental apartment. (At that time you would have to account for all of your previously deferred residence sale gains for tax purposes.) In this case, the exclusion would in effect be used to offset the accumulated gains attributable to several residences.

Another possibility to consider is the use of the one-time exclusion when you move to a less expensive home. The $125,000 exclusion in this case would offset that part of the gain that would not be covered by the rollover provision and would, therefore, otherwise be taxable.

Imputed Interest on Installment Sales of Land

Let's suppose you sell property, like a stamp collection, on the installment basis. Under the contract, you require 25 percent of the purchase price to be paid at the time of the sale and the balance payable in installments over five years.

The law assumes in such a situation that part of your installment proceeds are attributable to interest on the unpaid balance. Therefore, if no interest is stated in the sales contract or if only a minimal amount (say, 3 percent) is stated, the IRS will apply a 10 percent interest rate to the sale for tax purposes. This means that 10 percent of the gain on each installment payment will be taxed to you as interest. The balance will be capital gain.

The purpose of this law is to prevent you from transforming your interest income, which is taxed at the ordinary rates, into capital gain by forgoing interest in your contract in favor of increased total payments from the buyer.

The new law has adopted a 7 percent imputed interest rate (compounded semiannually) rather than the standard 10 percent for installment sales of land to related persons. "Related persons" include spouses, brothers and sisters, ancestors, and lineal descendants. However, the person cannot be a nonresident alien.

Another restriction is that to qualify for the 7 percent rate, the sales price cannot exceed $500,000. Moreover, the $500,000 amount is an aggregate limit that applies to all of your sales of land to relatives during the year. This means that you cannot avoid the restriction by selling the land in smaller pieces, each for less than $500,000.

Strategy Tip

The new law by its terms applies only to "land." It does not explain what happens when you sell land together with a house or other structure that is standing on it. Nothing in the law or in the congressional committee reports indicates that it would not apply in this case. However, in the future, the IRS may well take the position that the law can apply only to sales of vacant land.

So if you sell a building and the land under it to a relative on the installment method, charging no more than 7 percent interest, you may wish to protect yourself by making an allocation of the purchase price between the building and the land in accordance with their current market values. By doing this, you can at least preserve your right to claim that the portion of each installment payment attributable to the land should be covered by the 7 percent interest rate rather than the 10 percent rate rule.

4
Job Location

The 1981 law has created major new tax benefits for U.S. citizens and residents living abroad.

Foreign-Earned Income

Under the new law, you can, in 1982, elect to exclude and not report up to $75,000 of income earned abroad (Table 7). In 1983, the amount you can exclude from income is $80,000; in 1984, $85,000; in 1985, $90,000; and in 1986 and thereafter, the excludable amount is $95,000 of income earned abroad.

Table 7
PHASED INCREASES IN FOREIGN-EARNED-
INCOME EXCLUSION

Tax Year Beginning in	Amount
1982	$75,000
1983	80,000
1984	85,000
1985	90,000
1986 and later	95,000

What are the requirements to qualify?

To qualify for this special tax break, you must show that your principal place of work is located in a foreign country. You must also show that you have been a bona fide resident of the foreign country for an entire taxable year or for 330 days out of any consecutive twelve-month period. (This eligibility period is shorter than the 510 days out of any consecutive eighteen-month period that existed under the prior law.)

"Foreign-earned income" qualifying for the exclusion will generally be your earnings received in a foreign country (or countries) such as salary, fees, commissions, and the like. The exclusion does not extend to pension or annuity payments, interest, dividends, or income from passive sources. It also does not cover payments by the U.S. government or any of its agencies to an employee. As a general rule, then, the new exclusion is not available to any federal employees or members of the armed forces stationed abroad. However, the exclusion is available to certain individuals who are paid by the United States, such as teachers at certain schools abroad for U.S. dependents and some overseas independent contractors.

If you and your husband or wife qualify for the foreign-earned-income exclusion, it will be computed separately for both of you.

If you operate a business in a foreign country and capital is a material income-producing factor in the business, no more than 30 percent of the income from the business can be considered earned income from your labor.

How do you elect to use the exclusion?

The election is made on your tax return. Once made, your election will remain in effect for each subsequent year unless you notify the IRS that you want to revoke it. This is true even if you return to the United States and then move back abroad at a later time.

Once you revoke your election, however, you cannot reelect for five years. There is an exception if you get the consent of the IRS before you revoke.

How is the foreign tax credit affected by these changes?

If you earn income in a foreign country and are required to pay foreign taxes on it, the tax law permits you to claim a U.S. tax credit for the foreign taxes paid if the same income is also subject to U.S. tax. The purpose of the credit is to provide equal tax treatment for income earned at home and abroad. No credit is obviously available for amounts excluded under this provision.

However, it has not yet been made clear by the IRS how a person who has foreign earnings of more than the $75,000 excludable amount should compute the foreign tax credit.

For example, suppose Ted Lehmann earns $150,000 in a foreign country, all subject to foreign tax. The new provision will permit Ted to exclude $75,000 from his U.S. income. But he still has to pay U.S. taxes on the other $75,000. It is expected that Ted can still apply at least a portion of the foreign tax credit to his taxable $75,000. How he allocates the credit, however, is unclear. Look for IRS regulations to deal specifically with this point.

Is earned income the only exclusion?

If you qualify under these tests, the new law not only permits you to exclude the amounts of income earned abroad that are listed above but also gives you an additional exclusion for what is described as the "housing cost amount." The housing cost amount is the amount spent for housing expenses abroad for the taxable year less base amount equal to 16 percent of the salary of a GS-14, step-one U.S. employee. The latter component used in deriving the housing expense exclusion is computed on a daily basis for the revelent period. The housing exclusion applies to direct housing costs, to housing-related operating costs like insurance and utilities (but not interest and taxes), and, where applicable, to separate housing provided for your spouse and children if you must live or work in a dangerous or unhealthy location.

For example, assume during 1982 you earn $100,000 of foreign-earned income and spend $14,000 on housing costs. At the time the new law went into effect, the salary of a GS-14, step-one U.S. employee was $37,871. Sixteen percent of this amount is $6,059. You can now exclude $75,000 under the foreign-earned-income exclusion. In addition, you can exclude $7,941

31

($14,000 — $6,059) as additional housing-cost exclusion.

The new law provides that if you incur housing costs abroad during a year in which you either have no earnings abroad or in which your housing costs exceed your earnings abroad, you can carry those expenses forward one year and offset them against foreign-earned income of your next taxable year. In determining how much of the carried-forward housing expenses could be used in the next year, the carried-over amounts could be used only after the housing expenses incurred in that year.

For example, suppose Fred Rivera, a U.S. citizen, is a bona fide resident of a foreign country for all of 1983. Fred has no foreign earned income, and his housing cost amount (his foreign housing expenses over the base amount) is $30,000. Fred gets no exclusion for housing costs in 1983. In 1984, Fred has foreign-earned income of $150,000, and his housing cost amount is again $30,000. Fred would be entitled to an exclusion of $85,000 plus a deduction of his $30,000 housing cost amount paid in 1984. In addition, Fred would be permitted to deduct the $30,000 of his unused housing costs carried over from 1983.

Hardship camps

The 1981 law also retains, with some modifications, an exclusion existing under prior law for the value of housing or other lodging furnished to employees by their employers at "hardship camps." To qualify for the exclusion, the lodging must be furnished for the convenience of the employer and must be in a remote area where you, the taxpayer, would otherwise be unable to find satisfactory housing. It also must be located as close as possible to your place of work, in an area that is not available to the public at large, and it must accommodate ten or more employees.

5
Employee Benefits

The new law expands or extends the tax benefits available to employees from stock options, employee stock ownership plans, simplified employee pension plans, and group legal services plan. If you are an employee, you should be aware of the new rules so that you can improve your compensation package at the lowest tax cost. The same considerations are equally applicable if you are an employer. Knowledge of the new tax law can help you plan to keep employee morale high and still reduce the net cost of additional compensation.

Incentive Stock Options

Under the old law, the value of a stock option given to an employee was taxed as ordinary income if the option itself had a readily ascertainable fair market value when it was granted. If the option did not have a readily ascertainable value when granted, it was not taxed as ordinary income. Instead, when the employee exercised the option, the difference between the value of the stock at exercise and the option price was taxed as ordinary income to the employee. Such ordinary income at grant or exercise was treated as personal service income and taxed at a maximum rate of 50 percent. The employer, in turn, was entitled to a business expense deduction equal to the amount includable in the employees' income.

For example, suppose Frank Faithful works for Jones Plumbing. In recognition of his dedicated service, Mr. Jones gives Frank, as part of his compensation, an option to purchase 100 shares of company stock at $10 per share. At the time the option was granted, the stock was selling at $25 per share on the public exchange. Frank has ordinary income, and

33

Jones has a business deduction of $1,500 [(25 − 10) × 100]. If the option cannot be valued at the time it was granted and Frank later exercises it when the stock is selling at $30 per share, Frank has ordinary income, and Jones has a business deduction of $2,000 [(30 − 10) × 100].

How does the new law change the ground rules?

The new law generally restores the tax treatment of employee stock options to the law applicable prior to 1976. Under the new law, special tax treatment is given to "incentive stock options". There are no tax consequences when an incentive stock option is granted or when the option is exercised. Instead, the employee will be taxed at capital gains rates when and if he sells at a gain the stock received on the exercise of the option. Similarly, the employer gets no business expense deduction in connection with his granting of an incentive stock option.

Suppose Leslie Loyal receives a two-year qualified incentive stock option to buy 100 shares of her employer's stock at $50 a share. At the time she is given the option, the stock is selling for $50 a share. After $1^{1}/_{2}$ years, the stock goes up to $60 and she exercises the option. At this point, Leslie has no tax consequences. After another 5 years, Leslie sells the stock for $65. Leslie will have a $1500 long-term capital gain in the year of sale.

What is an "incentive stock option?"

The term "incentive stock option" means an option granted to an individual, for any reason connected with his employment, by the employer corporation or a related company, to purchase stock of any such corporations.

To receive incentive stock option treatment, the new law provides that the employee must not dispose of the stock within two years after the option is granted, and must hold the stock itself for at least one year. If all requirements other than these holding period rules are met, the tax will be imposed on the sale of the stock, but gain will be taxed as ordinary income rather than capital gain, and the employer will be allowed a deduction at that time.

What are the conditions for an incentive stock option?

For an option to qualify as an "incentive stock option," the following conditions must be met:

- The option must be granted under a plan specifying the number of shares of stock to be issued and the employees or class of employees to receive the option. This plan must be approved by the stockholders of the corporation within twelve months before or after the plan is adopted.
- The option must be granted within ten years of the date that the plan is adopted or the date that the plan is approved by the shareholders, whichever is earlier.
- The option must by its terms be exercisable only within ten years of the date it is granted.
- The option price must equal or exceed the fair market value of the stock at the time the option is granted. This requirement will be considered to be satisfied if there has been a good-faith attempt to value the stock accurately, even if the option price is less than the stock value.
- The option by its terms must be nontransferable other than at death and must be exercisable during the employee's lifetime only by the employee.
- The employee must not, immediately before the option is granted, own stock representing more than 10 percent of the voting power or value of all classes of stock of the employer corporation or its parent or subsidiary. However, the stock ownership limitations will be waived if the option price

is at least 110 percent of the fair market value (at the time the option is granted) of the stock subject to the option and the option by its terms is not exercisable more than five years from the date it is granted.

- The option by its terms is not to be exercisable while there is outstanding any incentive stock option that was granted to the employee at an earlier time. An option that has not been exercised in full is outstanding for the period that under its initial terms it could have been exercised.

  For this purpose, an option that has not been exercised in full is outstanding for the period that under its initial terms it could have been exercised. Thus, the cancellation of an earlier option will not enable a subsequent option to be exercised any sooner. Also, an option is considered to retain its original date of grant even if the terms of the option or the plan are later amended to qualify the option as an incentive stock option.

- In the case of options granted after 1980, the terms of the plan must limit the amount of aggregate fair market value of the stock (determined at the time of the grant of the option) for which any employee may be granted incentive stock options in any calendar year to not more than $100,000 plus the carry-over amount. The carry-over amount from any year after 1980 is one-half of the amount by which $100,000 exceeds the value (at time of grant) of the stock for which incentive stock options were granted in such prior year. Amounts may be carried over three years. Options granted in any year use up the $100,000 current-year limitation first and then the carry-over from the earliest year.

Strategy Tip

If your corporation wants to grant an employee options with total values more than $100,000, identify

$100,000 as incentive stock options and give the remainder in the form of separate non-statutory options. The congressional committee reports suggest that only incentive stock options will be taken into account for purposes of the $100,000 limit. The IRS may clarify this point in future regulations.

The new law provides that stock acquired on exercise of the option may be paid for with stock of the corporation granting the option. The difference between the option price and the fair market value of the stock at the exercise of the option will not be an item of tax preference.

Additional cash or other property may be transferred to the employee at the time the option is exercised so long as such property is subject to inclusion in income in accordance with its value.

An option will not be disqualified because of the inclusion of any condition not inconsistent with the qualification requirements.

The new law will apply to options granted after January 1, 1976, and exercised after December 31, 1980, or outstanding on such later date.

However, in the case of options (including qualified options) granted before January 1, 1981, an option is an incentive stock option only if the employer elects such treatment for an option. The aggregate value (determined at time of grant) of stock for which any employee may be granted incentive stock options prior to 1981 shall not exceed $50,000 per calendar year and $200,000 in the aggregate.

In the case of an option granted after January 1, 1976, and outstanding on the date of enactment, the option terms (or the terms of the plan under which the option was granted) may be changed, or shareholder approval obtained, to conform to the incentive stock option rules within one year of the date of enactment without the change giving rise to a new option requiring the setting of an option price based on a later valuation date. In conforming a prior option to an incentive stock option, you should be aware that your company will lose the deduction. Your desire to benefit the employee may override the desire for the deduction. In addition, even an exercised stock option will qualify as an incentive stock options if its terms happen to meet the new law's requirements.

All such changes relate back to the time of granting the original option. For example, if the option price of a ten-year option granted in 1978 is increased during the one year after date of enactment to 100 percent (110 percent, if applicable) of the fair market value of the stock on the date the option was granted in 1978, the price requirement will be met. Likewise, if the term of an option held by a 10 percent shareholder is shortened to five years from the date the option was granted, the 10 percent stock ownership limitation will not apply.

Employee Stock Ownership Plans (ESOP)

Since 1979, Congress has provided that corporate employees can be eligible for a tax credit based on contributions to an employee pension plan that is designed to invest primarily in the common stock of the employer. These plans are regularly called employee stock ownership plans (ESOPs). An ESOP must not allocate more than one-third of the corporation's contributions to officers, more-than-10 percent shareholders, and highly paid employees. Under the old law, the credit was based on a percentage of investment in the plan. As a result, many labor-intensive corporations were prevented from establishing such plans.

The new law opens the way for labor-intensive corporations to establish ESOPs by terminating the present investment-based tax credit for ESOP contributions and replacing it with a payroll-based tax credit after 1982. The payroll-based credit is allowed for wages paid during 1983–1987. For 1983 and 1984, the credit is limited to 0.5 percent of compensation paid to employees under the plan; it is limited to 0.75

percent of such compensation for 1985, 1986, and 1987. The credit is limited to the sum of (1) the corporations's first $25,000 of tax liability plus (2) 90 percent of the liability over $25,000.

The new law liberalizes the rules that allow an employer to deduct contributions to an ESOP that borrows to purchase the employer's stock. The deduction for the payment of principal and interest are allowed separately as deductions. The deduction for contributions for loan principal is limited to 25 percent of the compensation of all employees under the ESOP. The deduction for interest is unlimited.

Under the present law, an employee must be entitled to vote the stock allocated to his account under a deferred contribution plan. The new law abolishes the voting requirement with respect to profit-sharing plans for securities acquired after 1979. The voting requirement continues to apply to other plans in which participants can define their individual accounts.

Simplified Employee Pension Plans

A simplified employee pension plan (SEP) works like an IRA described in Chapter 6. The major difference is that the employee *and* his employer may contribute to a SEP.

If your employer sets up a SEP for you, you pay no tax on his contributions to the plan. Although the law requires you to report your employer's contributions in income, it also permits you to claim an offsetting deduction. Hence, the net tax effect is zero.

The employer's contributions to SEP are subject to the same rules applicable to Keogh plans (H.R. 10) for self-employed individuals (Table 8). The employee's contributions to a SEP are subject to the IRA rules. Therefore, the increases in the limits for contributions by self-employed individuals to pension plans and by employees to IRA accounts affect the contribution limits to a SEP by employers and employees.

Table 8
SEP RULES APPLICABLE IN 1981 AND 1982

	1981	1982
Employer's maximum contribution	Lesser of $7,500 or 15% of employee's compensation	Lesser of $15,000 or 15% of employee's compensation
Employee's maximum contribution	Lesser of $1,500 or 15% of employee's compensation compensation	Lesser of $2,000 or 100% of employees compensation compensation

An example of how this works is as follows: John Hicks earns $60,000 from his job at Acme Trucking Company, which establishes a SEP in 1981. In 1981, Acme can contribute $7,500 to the SEP on his behalf, and John can contribute $1,500. John pays no tax on the $7,500 and gets a deduction for his $1,500 contribution. In 1982, Acme can contribute $9,000 (60,000 × 15 percent) to the SEP, and John can contribute $2,000 to the SEP.

In addition, John can set up his own IRA in 1982 and get an additional tax deduction equal to a maximum of $2,000.

Group Legal Service Plans

For years, employers have contributed to group medical plans and group life insurance programs for employees almost as a matter of course. These payments do not constitute income to the employee by reason of special statutory provisions.

More recently, employer contributions to (and benefits provided under) a qualified group *legal* service plan have also been excluded from an employee's income, but this law was scheduled to expire on December 31, 1981. Now the new law extends it through December 31, 1984, so that like medical and group life insurance, group legal fees will not be includable in the employee's income.

6
Savings Incentives

The 1981 tax law creates a variety of new tax incentives to encourage savings. These changes include tax-exempt savings certificates, partial exclusion of interest and dividends, liberalization of the rules governing pension and retirement plans, and ESOPs.

All-Savers Certificates

One of the major changes of the 1981 tax law is the creation of the All-Savers Certificates, which offer an opportunity to earn interest income that is exempt from tax.

The new law grants a once-in-a-lifetime tax exemption to individuals of up to $1,000 ($2,000 on a joint return) of interest earned on a special new type of savings certificate that has been popularly called the All-Savers Certificate.

The new law provides that the $1,000 or $2,000 maximum exclusion applies to the total amount of interest paid on all tax-exempt savings certificates owned by the individual. The exclusion continues to be available until you reach the maximum. For example, if you only have enough funds to buy a certificate that will yield $600 in tax-free interest, you still have an unused exclusion of $400 that you can use in the future.

What is an All-Savers Certificate?

It is a certificate of deposit issued by a qualified savings institution, such as a bank, savings and loan association, or credit union, between September 30, 1981, and January 1, 1983. It must have a term of one year, must be made available at least in amounts of

$500, and must pay interest equal to 70 percent of the rate on fifty-two-week U.S. Treasury bills set monthly. The proceeds of the certificates must be used by the savings institution for residential financing.

Who should buy an All-Savers Certificate?

The new savings certificates don't make sense for everyone. To begin with, you pay a price for the tax break in the form of a lower interest rate. The special certificates can pay only 70 percent of the one-year Treasury bill rate. But if you're in a high enough tax bracket, the new savings certificates may be a good deal (Table 9).

Since the price for the tax benefit is 30 percent of the maximum possible yield on Treasury bills, the certificates will produce a net savings if your tax bracket exceeds 30 percent. For married couples in 1982, the certificates will benefit those couples whose taxable income (income less deductions and personal exemptions) exceeds $29,900. For single persons, the certificates will benefit those whose taxable income exceeds $23,500.

The following example may be helpful. On October 1, 1981, John Esposito, a single taxpayer, with 1981 taxable income of $13,000, is in the 26 percent bracket. He goes to the bank or savings and loan and discovers that the interest rate on fifty-two-week Treasury bills is 18 percent and the interest rate on All-Savers Certificates is 12.6 percent. If he purchases an All-Savers Certificate for $7,500, he will earn $945 in interest, which will be entirely free of federal tax. But if he had purchased an 18 percent money market certificate, he would have earned $1,350 in interest, on which he would have to pay a federal income tax of $351 ($1,350 × 26 percent) for a net yield of $999. Clearly, in this case, John's less-than-30-percent tax bracket makes the All-Savers Certificate a bad deal.

Suppose we assume that John Clark has a taxable

Table 9
EXAMPLES OF ALL-SAVER YIELDS*

Joint Taxable Income 1981	Your Maximum Tax Bracket (%)	12.61% for Taxable Equivalent Yields of	Single Individuals Taxable Income 1981	Your Maximum Tax Bracket (%)	12.61% for Taxable Equivalent Yields of
$29,901-35,200	37	20.02%	$18,201-23,500	34	19.11%
35,201-45,800	43	22.12%	23,501-28,800	39	20.67%
45,801-60,000	49	24.73%	28,801-34,100	44	22.52%
60,000-85,600	54	27.41%	34,101-41,500	49	24.73%

*Based on 70% of an average Treasury bill yield of 18.01%

43

income of $20,000, however, putting him in the 34 percent bracket. His $1,350 of Treasury bill interest would then be subject to $459 of income tax, leaving him only $891. The All-Savers Certificates, on the other hand, will still yield $945 for John. Here John's higher tax bracket makes the All-Savers Certificates a good deal by putting him ahead $54.

Strategy Tip

In determining whether to buy an All-Savers Certificate, you should also figure state income taxes into your calculation. Traditionally, interest earned on Treasury bills and other federal government instruments are not subject to state tax. However, whether the All-Savers Certificates will be exempt from state income taxes depends on whether your state income tax law follows the federal income tax law. If it does, the 1981 law automatically carries over into your state income tax, and the interest you earn from the All-Savers Certificates will also be exempt from state tax. For example, interest from All-Savers are exempt in New York, Maryland, and Virginia, but they are taxable in New Jersey and the District of Columbia. This is a question you should ask your local state income tax office.

What happens if you sell your All-Savers Certificate before maturity?

The new law states that if you redeem, sell, or pledge your All-Savers Certificate as collateral or security for a loan or withdraw any part of it, you lose the tax break on *all* the interest from the certificate. To get the tax savings, you have to lock up your money for a year. If you anticipate having cash needs over the year that may force you to redeem the certificate, you should probably not tie up your money in this way.

However, withdrawals of your earned interest on All-Savers are permitted. Of course, if you do withdraw the interest, you will earn a lower total amount over the term of the certificate because the compounding of the interest will be on a lesser amount.

Strategy Tip

If your financial picture makes early withdrawal a real possibility, purchase a number of All-Savers Certificates in different denominations to avoid losing the exemption on the entire amount.

What happens if interest rates continue to climb?

You should be aware that exempt savings certificates may not make sense as an investment for anyone in a market with rapidly rising interest rates. Thus, if interest rates continue to go up, the one-year certificate may be an unwise move.

This is especially true in view of the fact that as of January 1, 1982, the maximum tax on unearned income will go down from 70 percent to 50 percent. This means that all taxable income from investments (like taxable interest) will be taxed at a lower rate. Therefore, the tax break for All-Savers is less valuable in 1982 and later years to people whose income puts them in the 50–70 percent bracket for 1981.

The following example shows how rapidly climbing interest rates affect the value of the All-Savers tax break.

Suppose Mary Burke, a single taxpayer in the 50 percent bracket, purchases a $10,000 tax-exempt savings certificate on September 30, 1981, when interest rates on Treasury bills are 15 percent. The rate on the certificate will be computed as 10.5 percent (15 × .7), and Mary can therefore exclude $1,000 of the $1,050 interest earned. In this case, Mary would have an after-tax yield of $1,025 ($1,000 plus $50 subject to the 50 percent tax.)

Now suppose interest rates rise rapidly to 22 percent within the year. Mary could have purchased a

$10,000 Treasury bill and earned $2,200, which would be subject to a maximum tax of $1,100 (50 percent bracket), a better deal than the 10.5 percent tax savings certificate. Moreover, the Treasury bill is a fully liquid investment that can be sold at any time or pledged as security for a loan.

Therefore, the purchase of an All-Savers Certificate can be advantageous, but it is not necessarily the best investment for your dollar in all cases.

Should you borrow to buy an All-Savers?

It doesn't make sense to borrow funds to buy All-Savers. To begin with, you will be paying high interest to purchase lower-than-market-interest "certificates." Second, the interest you pay won't be tax deductible. The new law prohibits the deduction of interest paid to purchase All-Savers, just the way it also prohibits the deduction to purchase any tax-exempt investment.

What about package deals?

In August 1981, the newspapers were flooded with advertisements from banks and savings and loans offering bonus (taxable) interest rates on deposits (as much as 40 percent) for the month of September 1981 if the investors would commit themselves to reinvesting the proceeds into a tax-free All-Savers Certificate beginning October 1, 1981.

But the IRS soon threw cold water on this arrangement by announcing that such packages might threaten the tax break on the certificate. The IRS's position was that the (taxable) bonus and (nontaxable) certificate package could be viewed as a single loan offering, in violation of the new law, yielding interest greater than 70 percent of Treasury bills and for thirteen months instead of one year. Subsequently, on September 3, 1981, the IRS announced that banks and savings and loan associations could offer package deals linking high-interest bonuses with tax-free All-

46

Savers Certificates, but only if the links were optional. In practical terms, what they were saying was that to preserve your rights to the tax break on the All-Savers, the bank had to offer you the option of either reinvesting your money into an All-Savers Certificate or withdrawing your money and the accrued interest without penalty. If the reinvestment is optional, the IRS said, it would regard the bonus and the All-Savers as two separate deals, and the tax break would be preserved.

Strategy Tip

If you entered into a package deal prior to the IRS announcement, contact your bank or savings and loan. Although the IRS has no authority to grant retroactive relief to you, you may be able to have the bank conform the arrangement to the requirements of the law.

What denominations will the All-Savers Certificates come in?

The 1981 tax law states that All-Savers Certificates must be "made available in denominations of $500." But it doesn't say that other amounts, both lower and higher, won't be allowed as well.

On September 3, 1981, the government authorized banks and savings and loans to offer All-Savers in amounts lower or higher than $500. Thus, a bank or a savings and loan can offer them in denominations of $100, $1,000, or $2,000.

Also, the government will permit six-month money market certificates to be rolled over (reinvested) into All-Savers Certificates without penalty. Other time deposits, such as thirty-month certificates, can also be rolled over without penalty if the amount of time left in the original certificate is less than one year. Finally, the government has announced that a time-deposit certificate can be rolled over to an All-Savers only if its interest rate is higher than that on the All-Savers.

Strategy Tip

Any questions you have about shifting your time-deposit certificate to an All-Savers should be put to the IRS or a tax adviser before you act.

Checklist for All-Savers Certificates

- Determine your tax bracket. If you are in less than a 30 percent marginal bracket, the All-Savers are not for you. If you are in a higher bracket than 30 percent, the All-Savers may be a good deal.
- Determine your financial situation. Can you afford to lock up funds for a year? If not, the All-Savers are not for you. The penalty for early withdrawal (loss of the tax break), combined with the lower interest rate, is a financial disaster. Alternatively, consider buying several All-Savers in small denominations.
- Make the best estimate whether interest rates will rapidly rise during the one-year term of your All-Savers Certificate. While no one can predict trends in interest rates, look at the past few months' performance of the bond market. If you think that rates will skyrocket, you should think twice about investing in All-Savers.

Does taxable interest on All-Savers qualify for the $200 exclusion?

In 1980, Congress decided to permit taxpayers to exclude for 1981 and 1982 $200 per year of dividends and interest ($400 on a joint return no matter which spouse earns the dividends or interest). Congress has now cut back on the exclusion. It is still applicable for 1981, but it has been repealed for future years by the new law. For 1982 and later years, the $200/$400 exclusion drops to $100 per individual and is limited only to dividends.

You should note that no portion of any interest earned on an All-Savers Certificate is eligible for the $200 exclusion for 1981. This includes interest in excess of the $1,000/$2,000 limit on the All-Savers tax exemption or interest that is taxable because of a premature redemption.

Strategy Tip

Plan your purchases of All-Savers Certificates to ensure that you don't exceed the $1,000 or $2,000 maximum exclusion. There is no way under any other provision of the new law to avoid tax on any interest from these certificates in excess of the maximum allowable exclusion.

Therefore, keep a running tally of your purchases of All-Savers to make sure you don't exceed the $1,000/$2,000 lifetime limit. At current interest rates, a single taxpayer can purchase approximately $8,000 of All-Savers. For married persons filing jointly, the figure doubles to $16,000. However, if interest rates drop, the maximum investment goes up. For example, if interest rates fall to 10 percent, a single person will have to invest $10,000 and a married couple $20,000 to get the maximum tax benefit.

Also, plan your savings and stock investments for the remainder of 1981 to obtain the maximum benefits of the $200/$400 exclusion.

If you have a certificate of deposit coming due before the end of 1981 and have less interest than the $200/$400 maximum exclusion for that year, put the funds in a money market that pays interest on a daily basis to increase your 1981 interest income. Conversely, if you have more interest income than the 1981 maximum exclusion, consider switching from daily interest funds to term certificates if you can comfortably lock in the funds. You will at least postpone the tax.

Consider also selling off dividend-paying stock in 1982 if you have a loss that you can claim and if your dividends and interest exceed the $100 dividend and interest exclusion applicable for 1982, 1983, and 1984. Plan to increase your savings and stock investments in 1985 and thereafter to take advantage of the net-interest exclusion applicable for those years.

Net Interest

For the tax years following 1984, the new law creates a special exclusion for "net interest" (interest income less interest payments other than business and home mortgage interest). The new special exclusion is limited to a maximum of 15 percent of the lesser of (1) $3,000 ($6,000 on joint return) or (2) the taxpayer's net interest for the year. Thus, the maximum exclusion equals $450 (15 percent $\times$ $3,000) or $900 on a joint return.

The following example illustrates the mechanics of this provision. In 1985, Barbara Levi, a married taxpayer, has $6,000 of interest income and $3,000 of interest expenses (which include $2,000 of mortgage payments and $1,000 of miscellaneous nonbusiness interest, such as consumer loans and credit card finance charges). Her "net interest" is $5,000 ($6,000 − $1,000). Her interest exclusion on a joint return is computed as 15 percent of the lesser of $6,000 or $5,000, or $750. That means that only $5,250 of her $6,000 of interest income is subject to tax.

Note that not all interest income is eligible for the exclusion. There are six different categories of interest income that will qualify:

1. Interest on savings deposits
2. Interest on savings certificates
3. Interest on corporate bonds
4. Interest on otherwise taxable federal, state, or local obligations
5. Interest on participation shares in a trust established by a corporation
6. Interest paid by insurance companies on prepaid

premiums, policy proceedings, and policy holder dividends.

Strategy Tip

If you expect to have interest income in 1985 that is eligible for the exclusion, you should arrange to pay as much nonbusiness interest as you can in 1984 to avoid having it reduce your 1985 net interest exclusion.

The net interest exclusion is only reduced by non-business interest that is itemized as a deduction on your tax return. Thus, if you do not itemize deductions, you will be eligible for the maximum $450/$900 exclusion.

Public Utility Stock

For 1981-1985, the new law provides a special tax break for certain distributions to shareholders holding common stock in domestic public utilities, such as electric or gas companies. If the company provides you with the option of reinvesting cash dividends in common stock of the company and you do so, you may elect to exclude from tax up to $750 per year ($1,500 on a joint return) of the stock received. If you do elect to do this, the stock in your hands will have a tax "cost" of zero. This means that if you sell it, the proceeds will be fully taxable. If you sell the stock within a year, the gain will be classified as ordinary income. After one year, the gain will be taxed at the lower capital gains rate.

Strategy Tip

If you are considering buying public utility stock, check with your broker as to which utilities are adopting qualified dividends reinvestment plans.

Individual Retirement Accounts—IRA

In order to promote retirement saving, the law allows anyone who is a member of a qualified pension plan to take a tax deduction for contributions to the plan during the tax year. In addition, the law allows the earnings on the retirement savings to be tax free until you draw it out during your retirement years, but you must be at least 59½ years of age. Absent disability, if you draw funds out of your pension plan prior to age 59½, you not only will have to pay tax on the distribution but will also have to pay a 10 percent penalty. Withdrawals must begin by age seventy. The postponement of taxes and the ability of the pension plan to accumulate earnings tax free are very valuable benefits.

These pension plan rules therefore encourage you to put away your money for your retirement years and not to make an early withdrawal. Generally, these tax breaks result in permitting you to defer paying tax on some of your earnings during your high-income years and postponing it until your retirement years when you will probably be in a lower bracket.

In 1976, the tax laws began to allow individuals to start their individual own pension plans that qualified for the favored tax treatment. These plans are known as Individual Retirement Accounts, or IRAs. The 1981 tax act has significantly increased the benefits of an IRA and should make you seriously consider having one.

What is an IRA?

An IRA is a bank account or trust established for the exclusive benefit of an individual. The principal and interest that accumulate in an IRA can be distributed to the owner of the account for his or her retirement years. You can set up an IRA at almost any commercial bank or savings and loan. Where to go depends on which is paying the best interest. You can also appoint a trustee to manage your IRA in a brokerage account. However, the small amount involved makes a bank or savings and loan the most practical IRA trustee.

What are the new benefits?

Prior to 1982, the maximum annual tax deduction available for an IRA contribution was the smaller of (1) $1,500, (2) 15 percent of the taxpayer's annual compensation, or (3) the amount actually contributed. In addition, if you were a member of another pension or annuity plan or if you participated in a government retirement plan, you could not set up an IRA.

The new law provides two important changes in the IRA rules:

1. *Higher deductions for contributions.* For 1982 and thereafter, you can deduct on your income tax return a cash contribution to an IRA each year equal to the smaller of (1) $2,000 or (2) 100 percent of your yearly income. The time for making the contribution can be as late as April 15 of the following year when you file your return, or later if you obtain an extension to file.

   If your spouse works, both of you are eligible for a $2,000 deduction ($4,000 on a joint return). Moreover, even if your spouse does not work, you can still set up a "spousal IRA" and deduct up to $2,250 of contributions to it on a joint return. The contribution is divided between your IRA and your spouse's IRA. The deductible amount deposited to either account cannot exceed $2,000.

2. *Broadened eligibility.* Every individual, whether or not covered in another retirement or pension plan, can now have an IRA. This includes all government employees. This broadened eligibility is a major change from the old law.

How does an IRA benefit you tax-wise?

An IRA is, in many respects, one of the best tax shelters there is for middle-to-upper-income taxpayers. Everyone who can save $2,000 per year without having to draw upon it until age 59½ can claim a deduction for the amount contributed to the account.

Also, the interest income earned on this account is exempt from tax. As a result, your account will accumulate rapidly since its earnings are free of tax. Where else can you get a tax deduction for amounts deposited in a savings account?

You can also get the IRA deduction by making a voluntary contribution to your employee plan, if your plan permits this, by April 15 of the calendar year.

Strategy Tip

You should be careful what your IRA funds are invested in. Under the new law, an IRA that invests in "collectibles" after January 1, 1982 (for example, gold, art, stamps, gems, or antiques) is penalized by taxing you as if you received the amount invested as a distribution.

You should note that the new prohibition against IRA's investing in collectibles does not pose a serious disadvantage. There is no significant benefit to be gained by having your IRA purchase collectibles. The unrealized appreciation on a collectible owned by you is not subject to tax. And by putting collectibles in your IRA, you give up one of the principal benefits of an IRA—having interest income accumulate tax free.

These rules are illustrated in the following examples:

- Jake Gold is a federal government employee earning $30,000 per year. He is covered by a pension plan at work. For 1981, he cannot set up an IRA. But in 1982, he can set up an IRA and get a maximum tax deduction of $2,000 for a deposit. If he is married and his wife is not employed, he can set up a spousal IRA and deduct $2,250.

- Larry Johnson works for Jones Hardware and earns $8,000 per year. He has no pension plan. Mary, his wife, works as a teacher in the city school system for $15,000 per year. She has an employee-provided pension plan. For 1981, John can deduct an IRA contribution of $1,200 ($8,000 × 15 percent). Mary is ineligible for an IRA. For 1982, Larry can deduct $2,000, and Mary can also deduct $2,000, or $4,000 on a joint return. If either Larry or Mary direct the custodian of their IRA in 1982 or thereafter to buy an oriental rug for $4,000, that amount is immediately taxable.

Strategy Tip

If you're married, you should now maximize the benefits from the new IRA rules either by setting up a spousal IRA for a nonworking spouse, or by setting up a separate IRA to deduct the maximum amount allowable.

What about a divorced spouse?

Under the new law, a divorced spouse (or one separated under a decree of separate maintenance) for whom a spousal IRA had been established at least five years prior to the year of divorce and whose ex-spouse contributed to it for at least three of those five years can continue to make deductible contributions. However, the limit is $1,125 or the sum of the spouse's compensation and taxable alimony, whichever is less.

Strategy Tip

A divorced spouse who goes back to work may be better off setting up a new IRA to get the full $2,000 deduction.

Should you borrow to set up an IRA?

Normally, the interest paid on a loan to purchase a tax-exempt obligation, such as a municipal bond, is not deductible. However, there is nothing in the law or the regulations that appears to apply this principle to IRAs. The reason may be that the income earned in an IRA is not totally exempt from tax, just deferred into future years. Although the law is not altogether clear on this point, we know of no case in which the IRS has disallowed the interest on loans incurred to make contributions to an IRA. The contributions would, in any event, continue to be deductible.

Self-employed Individuals — Keogh Plans

The new law also increases the maximum allowable deduction for contributions by self-employed persons to their Keogh pension plans (Table 10).

Table 10
KEOGH PENSION PLANS

	1981	1982
Maximum contribution	Lesser of $7,500 or 15% of earnings from self-employment	Lesser of $15,000 or 15% of earnings from self-employment

For example, suppose Dr. Max Braun, a self-employed physician, earns $125,000 from his medical practice. For 1981, he can claim a maximum deduction of $7,500 as a contribution to his Keogh Plan. In 1982, the allowable maximum goes up to $15,000.

Strategy Tip

Like an employee who has an SEP, a self-employed individual who has a Keogh plan is also eligible to establish an IRA for 1982 and claim another $2,000 deduction for an IRA contribution.

Should you borrow from a Keogh plan?

Under the old law, if a sole proprietor of a business or a more-than-10-percent partner borrowed from or pledged his Keogh plan benefits, he was treated as having received a distribution from the plan in the amount of the loan or pledge. In these circumstances, he would be subject to a tax on the amount of the distribution plus a penalty equal to 10 percent of the distribution.

The new law extends this rule to all partners in a

partnership, whatever their interest, and to all loans made after 1981. The new loan rule does not apply to loans outstanding after December 31, 1981, as long as these loans are not renegotiated, extended, or revised after that date.

Employees of the partnership, who may be participants in an employee plan, are not subject to the loan rule. Therefore, they may continue to borrow or pledge their interest in the plan.

Strategy Tip

If you are a 10-percent-or-less partner with an interest in a Keogh plan and a loan from the plan outstanding as of December 31, 1981 and you find yourself unable to meet its terms, consider financing from another source to avoid the tax and 10 percent penalty that is triggered on renegotiation of the loan.

How about pension plans in Subchapter S corporations?

The tax law permits a certain type of small business corporation to choose to be taxed as if its shareholders were members of a partnership. This type of corporation is known as a Subchapter S corporation.

The rules applicable to pension plans of Subchapter S corporations are the same as those governing plans of self-employed persons. So for 1982 and after, Subchapter S corporations are subject to the new contribution limits and restrictions against borrowing that are applicable to self-employed pension plans.

Should you borrow to make a contribution to a Keogh plan?

See our earlier discussion as to borrowing to contribute to an IRA. The contributions would be deductible in the same manner as if you contributed your own funds to the plan.

Elimination of the "Made Available" Rule

Under the old law, once a retirement plan "made available" any portion of the money in an individual account, the individual was subject to taxation on the contribution whether or not he actually received it. The object of the "made available" rule was to prevent early withdrawal of funds. To protect the individual participant in a plan against tax liability of which he might be unaware, many plans called for stiff penalties—such as halting employer contributions—to deter early withdrawal from the retirement plans.

Under the new law, the fact that an amount in a plan is "made available" will not result in taxation of a participant until the amount is actually distributed.

The change is effective for tax years beginning after December 31, 1981.

7
The Internal Revenue Service

The cost of interest on delinquent taxes and underpayments as well as the actual cost of penalties are going up under the new law.

Interest Rate on Underpayments and Overpayments

The 1981 law makes it more costly for you to underpay your income tax. It does this by pegging the interest rate that the government can charge you for underpayments and delinquent taxes to the prime rate. Conversely, the increase works to your benefit for overpayments. In that case, the government will pay you the prime rate.

Here's how the new interest rate rule works. After October 1, 1981, the annual rate of interest for tax deficiency purposes will be set at the prime rate on October 15, 1981, and the rate will be formally adjusted as of February 1, 1982. The rate determined on October 15, 1982, will become effective as of January 1, 1983. This rule replaces the present law under which the rate was set at 90 percent of the adjusted prime rate, with adjustments limited to every two years.

Until February 1, 1982, the rate charged by the IRS will be 12 percent. Since the prime rate was about 20 percent when this book went to press, it is virtually certain that there will be an upward adjustment in the interest rate effective February 1, 1982.

Strategy Tip

If the IRS charges you with deficiency in tax after October 1, 1981, you should consider paying it before February 1, 1982 (if you don't contest it) to avoid the higher interest rate. The higher rate could be costly because interest is charged from the filing date of the return, not from the date your return is audited.

Penalties for False Withholding Information

When you begin a new job, your employer presents you with a W-4 Form to list your number of personal exemptions. This enables your employer to compute the income tax to be withheld from your wages.

In recent years, some people have attempted to avoid the withholding of income taxes from their wages by deliberately overstating their withholding exemptions. In order to combat this practice, the civil penalty for making false statements that cause a decrease in the amount of withholding has been increased from $50 to $500 under the new law.

The criminal penalty imposed for these false statements also is raised from $500 to $1,000.

Under current IRS practice, employers are required to report to the IRS all employees who claim more than nine withholding allowances. If you claim more than nine, you may be asked by the IRS to justify your need based on the number of your dependents and the amount of your deductions.

Negligence Penalty

The old law imposes a 5 percent penalty of any underpayment due to negligence or intentional disregard of rules and regulations.

The new law retains this 5 percent penalty and adds a further penalty of 50 percent of the interest due on the underpayment. The new penalty is not deductible as interest because the law calls it an "addition to tax" rather than interest, and only interest is deductible.

Penalty for Failure to File Information

Various individuals or entities, like banks, employers, and dividend-paying corporations, are required to file certain information returns with the federal government to assist it in ascertaining your income and collecting your taxes. These tax returns are really just information statements, describing various transactions, like the payment of certain amount of wages to the employees over the year or the dividends paid out to a corporation's shareholders. The IRS does not require the person or entity that files the reports to pay any taxes. A $10 penalty per income statement (with a maximum of $25,000 per year) is imposed on the person or entity charged with filing them for failure to do so.

The new law broadens the reach of this penalty. It now includes:

- dividends
- patronage dividends paid by cooperatives
- interest exceeding $10
- wage payments made by paying group term life insurance premium
- rents of $600 or more
- shares of catches of certain fishing boat crews
- W-2 statements of wages

Similar penalties are imposed for failure to provide the recipient of the payment with the required information return.

Penalty for Overstated Deposit Claims

Employers who withhold taxes for their employees' wages are required to deposit the withheld amounts in a federal depository, such as a bank. Failure to make the required payments results in a penalty.

The new law imposes an additional penalty for those employers who do not make the required deposits but falsely report that they have done so. The penalty will also be applied against employers who claim deposits in excess of the actual amount they have deposited. The new penalty is equal to 25 percent of the overstated deposit claim. Mistakes due to reasonable cause and not to willful neglect will not be penalized.

Penalty for Valuation Overstatements

There is a new penalty for "valuation overstatements" of property on income tax returns of individuals and certain types of corporations. For example, if you make a charitable contribution of property and then take a tax deduction overstating the property's value on your return, you will be charged a penalty if three conditions are met: (1) the overstatement exceeds 150 percent of the correct valuation; (2) the overstatement results in an underpayment of taxes of at least $1,000; and (3) the property was acquired within five years of the year for which the overstatement was made. This new penalty applies after December 31, 1981.

The penalty is equal to a percentage of the underpayment of tax that results from the overvaluation, in accordance with the graduated scale in Table 11.

Table 11
OVERVALUATION PENALTIES

If the valuation claimed is the following percentage of the correct valuation	The applicable penalty percentage is:
150–200	10
201–250	20
More than 250	30

This new penalty has a broad application. In addition to the situation of an overvalued charitable gift, it can likewise apply to the overvaluation of property (such as a building or equipment) for purposes of claiming depreciation deductions in a business, tax shelter, or other investment. And it can apply in other contexts as well.

Strategy Tip

This new law provides that the IRS may waive all or any part of the valuation penalty if you can prove that there was a reasonable basis for the claimed valuation and that your claim was made in good faith. Therefore, it is important to retain any documentation (appraisals, legal opinions, etc.) that might convince the IRS of your good faith in making the valuation.

Tax Court Filing Fee

One of the federal courts having jurisdiction to hear tax disputes between taxpayers and the IRS is the U.S. Tax Court. If you have a tax controversy that has proceeded to the stage a court contest, you can get a hearing in the Tax Court by filing a petition with the clerk's office.

The new law authorizes the Tax Court to increase the fee you will be charged for filing a petition from the existing $10 to a maximum of $60. The increase will be in effect for petitions filed after December 31, 1981.

Strategy Tip

For cases involving $5,000 or less for any one taxable year, the Tax Court has a special small-claims procedure. The procedure can be chosen at your option, and your case will be handled on a more informal level than if you seek regular review of your case. The only disadvantage, however, is that a small-claims decision cannot be appealed to a higher court if you lose. On the other hand, however, it can't be appealed by the government if you win. So, for a small case involving factual rather than legal questions, the small-claims route may be desirable.

At this writing, the Tax Court is considering retaining the $10 filing fee for cases under the small-claims procedure.

If you are planning to file a petition in the Tax Court in the next few months, you should try to file it before the end of the year to take advantage of the lower filing fee.

8
The Estate and Gift Tax

Background

The federal estate tax is a tax on the transfer of property at death. If you have an estate large enough to be subject to the tax, it affects all of your property (cash, houses, stocks and bonds, life insurance proceeds, etc.) that you own at death. The tax is measured by the value of the property you transfer to your heirs and beneficiaries (less exemptions and deductions), and the rates are graduated. There are various allowable deductions, including the marital deduction (for transfers to your spouse), the deduction for funeral and administration expenses, the deduction for charitable gifts, and the deduction for claims against the estate.

The federal estate tax also reaches certain types of lifetime transfers of property (or gifts) that the law considers to be like transfers made at death. Generally speaking, if you transfer property during your lifetime and retain control over the property so that the recipient does not have unlimited power over it, the value of the property will be subject to tax in your estate.

There are also various credits that can be applied against the tax due. These include (1) the credit for state death taxes, (2) the credit for foreign death taxes, and most importantly, (3) the "unified credit," which is explained in Table 12.

There have been many changes in this law governing estate and gift taxes over the years, and in order to appreciate the dramatic changes that the 1981 law makes, it is helpful to know this background. Prior to 1976, there was a $60,000 estate tax exemption for all estates. Therefore, only estates with assets in excess of $60,000 were subject to the estate tax. In 1976, the

Table 12
PHASE-IN OF THE UNIFIED CREDIT UNDER THE 1976 LAW

For persons dying in:	The unified credit is:	"Exemption equivalent"
1977	$30,000	$120,000
1978	34,000	134,000
1979	38,000	147,333
1980	43,500	161,563
1981	47,000	175,625

$60,000 exemption (as well as a separate $30,000 exemption for gifts) was replaced with a tax credit that could be applied either to the tax on lifetime transfers (e.g., gifts) or transfers at death.

Then, in 1976, Congress discarded the estate and gift tax exemptions in favor of the "unified credit." The unified credit was to be phased in over a five-ear period. The original schedule is shown in Table 12.

The "exemption equivalent" is the equivalent-sized estate that would be exempt from tax under an exemption rather than a credit method of figuring the tax. For example, anyone dying in 1981 could have made lifetime gifts and transfers upon their death equal to $175,625 without incurring any estate or gift taxes. This is substantially more than the old $60,000 estate and $30,000 gift tax exemption.

The new law changes the tax considerably.

Increase in the Unified Credit

First and foremost, the new law continues the upward-phased annual increases in the unified credit from the present $47,000 to $192,800 over the next six years. This is an increase of over 400 percent.

The increases are outlined in Table 13.

Therefore, after 1986, you will be able to transfer a total of $600,000 to anyone, either during your lifetime or by will at your death, without having to pay any tax.

Table 13
PHASE-IN OF THE UNIFIED CREDIT UNDER THE NEW LAW

For persons dying in:	The unified credit will be:	"Exemption equivalent"
1982	$ 62,800	$225,000
1983	79,300	275,000
1984	96,300	325,000
1985	121,800	400,000
1986	155,800	500,000
1987 and after	192,800	600,000

Strategy Tip

You should immediately review the size of your taxable estate, keeping in mind the increased unified credit. If your estate, is equal to or less than $225,000 in 1982 or will be no greater than $600,000 in 1987, you can dispose of your assets in any manner that you wish without worrying about the estate tax.

Will your estate need to file an estate tax return?

The phased increases in the unified credit reduces the number of estates that are required to file estate tax returns because the size of an estate for which an estate tax return must be filed is much larger now. Therefore, for anyone dying in 1982, an estate tax return must be filed only if their assets at death exceed $225,000. Of course, this figure increases in stages to $600,000 for 1987 and later.

Strategy Tip

Review your insurance policies. Many people maintain some life insurance policies in order to have enough cash available so their estate tax bill can be covered at the time of their death. Some persons have assigned life insurance policies to keep the proceeds out of their taxable estate. These policies and practices may no longer be necessary now that the estate tax will affect fewer estates. If you already have enough life insurance to provide for your loved ones if you die, you may wish to phase out your excess insurance in step with increases in the unified credit.

Estate Tax Rate Cuts

The estate tax rates under the old law are listed in Table 14.

Table 14
OLD LAW

If the Estate and the Taxable Gifts Amount to:	Then the Tax is:
Not over $10,000	18% of such amount
Over $10,000 but not over $20,000	$1,800, plus 20% of the excess of such amount over $10,000
Over $20,000 but not over $40,000	$3,800, plus 22% of the excess of such amount over $20,000
Over $40,000 but not over $60,000	$8,200, plus 24% of the excess of such amount over $40,000
Over $60,000 but not over $80,000	$13,000, plus 26% of the excess of such amount over $60,000
Over $80,000 but not over $100,000	$18,200, plus 28% of the excess of such amount over $80,000
Over $100,000 but not over $150,000	$23,800, plus 30% of the excess of such amount over $100,000
Over $150,000 but not over $250,000	$38,800, plus 32% of the excess of such amount over $150,000
Over $250,000 but not over $500,000	$70,800, plus 34% of the excess of such amount over $250,000

If The Estate and the Taxable Gifts Amount to:	Then the Tax is:
Over $500,000 but not over $750,000	$155,800, plus 37% of the excess of such amount over $500,000
Over $750,000 but not over $1,000,000	$248,300, plus 39% of the excess of such amount over $750,000
Over $1,000,000 but not over $1,250,000	$345,800, plus 41% of the excess of such amount over $1,000,000
Over $1,250,000 but not over $1,500,000	$448,300, plus 43% of the excess of such amount over $1,250,000
Over $1,500,000 but not over $2,000,000	$555,800, plus 45% of the excess of such amount over $1,500,000
Over $2,000,000 but not over $2,500,000	$780,800, plus 49% of the excess of such amount over $2,000,000
Over $2,500,000 but not over $3,000,000	$1,025,800, plus 53% of the excess of such amount over $2,500,000
Over $3,000,000 but not over $3,500,000	$1,290,800, plus 57% of the excess of such amount over $3,000,000
Over $3,500,000 but not over $4,000,000	$1,575,800, plus 61% of the excess of such amount over $3,500,000
Over $4,000,000 but not over $4,500,000	$1,880,800, plus 65% of the excess of such amount over $4,000,000
Over $4,500,000 but not over $5,000,000	$2,205,800, plus 69% of the excess of such amount over $4,500,000
Over $5,000,000	$2,550,800, plus 70% of the excess of such amount over $5,000,000

The *new law* reduces the maximum 70 percent estate tax rate to 50 percent, phased in over the next four years. The reductions are in 5 percent increments (Table 15).

Table 15
NEW LAW

For 1982—for persons dying and gifts made in 1982, the applicable rate is:

Amount	Tax
Over $2,500,000 but not over $3,000,000	$1,025,800, plus 53% of the excess over $2,500,000
Over $3,000,000 but not over $3,500,000	$1,290,800, plus 57% of the excess over $3,000,000
Over $3,500,000 but not over $4,000,000	$1,575,800, plus 61% of the excess over $3,500,000
Over $4,000,000	$1,880,800, plus 65% of the excess over $4,000,000

For 1983—for persons dying and gifts made in 1983, the applicable rate is:

Amount	Tax
Over $2,500,000 but not over $3,000,000	$1,025,800, plus 53% of the excess over $2,500,000
Over $3,000,000 but not over $3,500,000	$1,290,800, plus 57% of excess over $3,000,000
Over $3,500,000	$1,575,800, plus 60% of excess over $3,500,000

For 1984—for persons dying and gifts made in 1984, the applicable rate is:

Amount	Tax
Over $2,500,000 but not over $3,000,000	$1,025,800, plus 53% of the excess over $2,500,000
Over $3,000,000	$1,290,800, plus 55% of the excess over $3,000,000

For 1985 and thereafter—for persons dying and gifts made in 1985 and thereafter, the applicable rate is:

Amount	Tax
Over $2,500,000	$1,025,800, plus 50% of the excess over $2,500,000

Strategy Tip

Whatever the size of your estate, you should immediately review your will to make sure that its provisions are not tied to the old estate-tax law and rate structure. For example, you may have certain charitable bequests in your will designed solely to save estate taxes. These bequests may no longer be necessary in light of the unified credit and the new rates.

Increase in Annual Gift Tax Exclusion

Prior to the new law, the gift tax law permitted you to make an unlimited number of $3,000 gifts each year free of any gift tax and without consuming any exemption or credit. This provision in the gift tax is called the "annual exclusion" or the "per donee" exclusion.

In the new 1981 law, Congress increased the annual exclusion to $10,000, effective for all gifts made after 1981.

Now you can make as many gifts of $10,000 or less each year to as many different people as you like and not be subject to any gift tax. In making these gifts, you don't use up any of your unified credit.

In addition, if your spouse joins you in giving gifts, you can double the gift tax exclusion and make an unlimited number of $20,000 gifts per year.

Strategy Tip

Consider making annual gifts to your children of $10,000 (or $20,000 with your spouse) to fund their education. The gifts are free of the gift tax and will reduce the assets in your estate at your death. In addition, your children will not have to pay income tax on the transfers because they are gifts. Subsequently, when the money is invested, the children will probably pay less income tax on the accumulated interest earned because they will be in a lower income tax bracket than you or your spouse.

Since the annual gift tax exclusion is generally limited to gifts of "present interests" (i.e., outright gifts of cash or property), in making gifts, be sure not to attach any strings if you want to come within the $10,000 exclusion.

There is an exception to the present interest requirement for a gift to a trust for the benefit of a minor where the property and income given may be used to benefit the minor before he or she reaches twenty-one and will, to the extent it is not used, be transferred to the minor at age twenty-one. This type of trust-known as Section 2503(c), Gift to Minors Trust-can be easily set up at any bank or savings and loan and qualifies for the gift tax exclusion. It is therefore a perfect way to give tax-free gifts to young children. Your local bank or savings and loan will be glad to help you with the paperwork.

Unlimited Gift Tax Exclusion for Amounts Paid for Tuition or for Health Care

Under the new law, you can make unlimited gifts to a school for tuition for a particular person or to a health-care provider for medical care for a particular person. These gifts will be tax free.

The exclusion for medical expenses (including medical insurance) applies only to direct payments made by you to the physician or the organization providing the medical services (i.e., you can't get the tax break by reimbursing the person who received the medical services).

However, the unlimited exclusion is not permitted for any payments that are reimbursed by insurance. For example, if you pay for your nephew's medical expenses and your nephew also receives insurance reimbursement, your payment (to the extent of the reimbursement) is not eligible for the unlimited gift tax exclusion. And this is true whether or not the reimbursement is paid in the same or subsequent year.

As for educational expenses that you might pay on behalf of your grandchild, for example the unlimited gift tax exclusion is limited to direct payments to the school. The exclusion can be applied to both full- and part-time students, but it is limited to direct tuition costs. Therefore, books, supplies, dormitory fees, and the like are not covered.

In providing an unlimited gift tax exclusion for certain medical expenses and tuition, Congress did not intend to change the law that states that you cannot consider medical expenses or tuition a gift if the person paying is under a legal obligation (such as a child-support decree or a parental duty) to provide these items to the recipient. These payments are not gifts; therefore, the applicability of the gift tax exclusion never arises.

Unlimited Marital Deduction

One of the most revolutionary changes brought about by the 1981 tax law is the establishment of an unlimited estate tax marital deduction.

Under the new law, after 1981, there is no longer any dollar ceiling on the estate and gift tax marital deduction for the estates of people dying and for gifts made to spouses. This means you can now transfer unlimited amounts of your property tax free to your spouse either during your lifetime or upon your death.

The unlimited marital deduction represents a generous revision in the estate tax. Under the old law, the maximum estate tax marital deduction for property passing to your spouse was limited to $250,000, or one-half of your adjusted gross estate, whichever was larger. The old law also provided a gift tax marital deduction for the first $100,000 of gifts to a spouse. The second $100,000 of gifts to a spouse was fully taxable. Gifts in excess of $200,000 were eligible for a 50 percent deduction. Those dollar limits are now a thing of the past.

Strategy Tip

The new law contains a transitional rule that makes prompt review and revision of your will imperative. If your will leaves property to your spouse under a

72

formula limiting the value of the bequest to an amount no greater than the old marital deduction (the greater of $250,000 or one-half the estate), the new tax law presumes that you did not intend to have the new unlimited marital deduction apply. While you may be satisfied that your will is adequate, you owe it to yourself and your family to make that decision again in light of the new law.

How can you use the new marital deduction provision to best advantage in planning your estate?

One way to take advantage of the unlimited marital deduction may be to leave your entire estate outright to your spouse. If you do (assuming, of course, that you die before your spouse), you can absolutely ensure that your estate will pass tax free no matter whether it is $600,001 or $6 billion. But whether this is wise tax planning for you requires consideration of a number of other factors, including the amount of your spouse's existing estate, your spouse's needs, and the needs of your children or others whom you may wish to benefit.

Since the estate tax rates are graduated, it may not make sense to leave your entire estate to your spouse if your spouse already has substantial assets and does not need the property because all of the property will be in your spouse's estate at death, requiring payment of an even heavier tax than if you had paid tax on your share. Thus, if you and your spouse are both independently wealthy and do not need the assets of the other spouse, it may be desirable for you to forgo the benefits of the unlimited marital deduction and to leave portions of the estate to your children or others. This technique avoids overloading the second estate and should at least be utilized to the extent of the unified credit.

For example, suppose Ben Simon has a taxable estate of $1.2 million and dies after 1985. He leaves his entire estate to his wife Jane. Ben's estate pays no estate tax upon his death because of the unlimited marital deduction. If the $1.2 million is still intact in Jane's estate at her death, her estate will pay $246,000 in estate taxes. If Ben had left $600,000 to his children and $600,000 to Jane, he would have paid no estate tax upon his death because of the marital deduction and the unified credit. When Jane dies, if the $600,000 she received is still intact (assuming she has no other assets), she will pay no estate tax because of the unified credit. Thus, a net saving of $246,000 can be achieved by splitting the estate.

Strategy Tip

If you and your spouse are both wealthy and will have estate tax consequences at death, it may make sense for you to immediately begin a program of making annual $20,000 gifts to each of your children or others who will benefit at your death under your will. These gifts are subject to the annual exclusion and are thus free of gift tax. They also do not use up any part of your unified credit. If you have two children, $40,000 per year can be given away.

• Splitting the estate between your spouse and others is only desirable if the surviving spouse does not need all of the assets to live on. If your spouse is much younger than you, disabled, has no independent source of income, or for other reasons may need all of your assets at your death, you should factor this consideration into your estate plan.

Can a trust qualify for the marital deduction?

The new marital deduction provisions also include a related liberalizing provision that now allows certain trusts to qualify for the marital deduction. Trusts covered by this new provision are those in which the income from the trust property is paid to the spouse for life and at the spouse's death the trust property goes to children or other beneficiaries.

Under prior law, such trusts did not qualify for the

marital deduction because they gave the surviving spouse only a "terminable interest" in the property. Prior law required that to qualify for the marital deduction in the estate of the first spouse to die, the property had to be subject to estate tax in the estate of the surviving spouse so that at least one tax would be paid at that generational level. A "life interest" in a trust, as described above, is not in general an asset in the second spouse's estate at death because the interest is extinguished at death and the spouse does not control the transfer to subsequent beneficiaries.

Under the new law, such trusts can qualify for the marital deduction. The "price" for this provision is that the so-called terminable interest property must be included in the surviving spouse's estate at his or her death. Therefore, the trust property will be taxed at that time. In addition, if it is transferred during the life of the beneficiary spouse, it will be subject to gift taxes.

The requirements of the new provision are (1) that the income be paid to the surviving spouse at least annually for life and (2) that no person can have the power to transfer the property to any person other than the surviving spouse during his or her lifetime. If you wish to claim this, you will have to file an election with the IRS.

There are certain limitations, however; Income paid by a trust for a set term of years or a life interest that will be cut off by the spouse's remarriage (or any other condition) will not qualify for the marital deduction. Therefore, if you want to exact a financial penalty upon your surviving spouse for remarriage, your estate will pay an estate tax price in the form of a forfeited marital deduction.

The new trust rule can be illustrated by the following example. Suppose Ben Simon leaves $600,000 outright to Jane and puts $600,000 in a trust, in our earlier example, the income of which is payable to her at least annually during her lifetime, with the principal paid over to their children upon her death. Ben

would pay no estate tax because the entire estate would qualify for the marital deduction. On Jane's death, the trust would be part of her taxable estate and subject to estate tax. But if the $600,000 remained intact, it would pass to her heirs free of tax because of the unified credit. Jane's estate tax would again be $246,000.

Strategy Tip

Keep in mind that estate taxes are only one item to consider in planning the disposition of your estate. It may well be that your spouse is involved in income-producing activities that require the unrestricted use of capital. In this case, it might be unwise to split up your estate between your spouse and other beneficiaries or to create a restrictive trust that would interfere with those activities simply to save estate taxes. If your entire estate can be put to productive use by your spouse, the estate-tax savings on your spouse's death may not be that important. This point is especially true in light of the fact that by 1985, the maximum estate tax rate will be cut to 50 percent.

Other factors should be considered, too. Is your estate mostly made up of assets that are not liquid—like a major art collection or stock in a family corporation or small business—that would have to be sold to pay the estate tax?

If you take advantage of the unlimited marital deduction, you can postpone the tax until your spouse dies, which may be in your best interest, even if it risks overloading your spouse's estate. Postponing the tax also gives you the use of the tax money in the interim and the interest it earns, another consideration to keep in mind if you are looking at a big estate tax bill.

Community Property

In some states (e.g., California, Louisiana, Texas), spouses own property in a special joint status known as "community property."

Under the new tax law, transfers of community property between spouses are now eligible for the estate and gift tax marital deduction.

Jointly Held Property

Under the new law, where property is held jointly by husband and wife, with the right of survivorship (i.e., when one of the co-owners dies, the other automatically becomes the owner of all of the property), one-half the value of this property is the amount that will be included in the estate of the first spouse to die. This is a change from the old law, which made includability dependent on which spouse paid for the property. The new rule is effective for the estates of persons dying after 1981. The new law eliminates questions that previously arose as to reconstructing the contributions made by both spouses in paying for the property.

For example, Alan and Helen Farmer own a house purchased in 1950 for $40,000 that is now worth $200,000. On December 31, 1981, Alan dies. Under the old law, unless Alan's estate could show that Helen paid for part of the house, the entire $200,000 was includable in his gross estate and could therefore be taxed. If Alan dies on January 1, 1982, when the new law takes effect, only $100,000, one-half the value of the house, will be includable in his gross estate.

However, this new law may prove disadvantageous if, after Alan's death, Helen wishes to sell the house. Suppose Helen sells the house for $240,000 in 1983 and moves into an apartment in town. Her "tax cost" (basis) under the old law (for purposes of figuring the amount of her gain on the sale) would have been $200,000, the value of the house at the time of her husband's death. Therefore, if Helen sold the house for $240,000, she would have to pay a capital gains tax (maximum 20 percent) on $40,000. Under the new law, however, her "tax cost" will only be $120,000 ($100,000 included in Alan's estate) plus $20,000 (half of the original cost). In a $200,000 sale, she would have a capital gain of $120,000 and a tax bill of $24,000. (20 percent × $120,000).

Strategy Tip

If the parties have a trusting relationship, consider eliminating all jointly held property (stocks, bonds, houses, etc.) and put this property in the hands of the spouse most likely to die first. At the death of the first spouse, the property can pass to the surviving spouse free of estate tax because of the marital deduction. More importantly, the surviving spouse will take the property at a higher "tax cost" for income tax purposes.

You should note that if later Helen wants to sell the house, she should consider using the residence roll-over rules discussed in Chapter 3.

Transfers Made Within Three Years of Death

Under prior law, the value of property transferred by a person within three years of his death was included in his taxable estate. The new law abolishes the three-year rule for outright transfers. For people dying after 1981, the new law provides that gifts made within three years of death are not included in the taxable estate.

Charitable Gifts of Copyrighted Art Works

Under the old law, it was generally impossible to obtain an estate tax charitable deduction for donation of a work of art if you didn't also donate the copyright.

The new law provides that when you contribute a copyrightable work of art to a charity as part of your will, the work of art and the copyright will be treated as separate properties for purposes of the estate tax charitable deduction. In other words, a charitable deduction will be allowable for the transfer of a work of art to charity, whether or not the copyright itself is simultaneously transferred to the charity.

Installment Payment of Estate Taxes

The new law consolidates the provisions permitting the payment of estate taxes installments where a principal asset of the estate is an interest in a family or other business.

The new provisions are applicable for persons dying after 1981 and where the value of the business exceeds 35 percent of the gross estate. In these cases, the estate taxes attributable to the interest may be deferred for up to fourteen years! If the business is worth less than $1 million, interest only at a bargain 4 percent rate is payable for the first four years with the balance of the principal and interest payable over the next ten years.

If more than 50 percent of the business is sold or disposed of in some other way before the estate tax payments are completed, the unpaid tax is immediately due. Dispositions to your family do not count for this purpose. A delinquent payment to IRS for six months or more will also cause the balance of the unpaid taxes to be due immediately. Late installment payments made within six months will trigger penalties but not immediate payment of the tax.

Payment of Gift Taxes

Under the new law, gift tax returns and gift taxes are now due on an annual (rather than quarterly) basis on April 15 of the year after the gift was made. However, if the donor dies during the year he or she gave the gift, then the gift tax return is due at the same time as the donor's estate tax return (with extensions).

Disclaimers of Property

Prior to the 1981 law, the steps you had to take to refuse a bequest of property under a will or trust (so that the property simply passed to the next person in line) were not altogether clear. In some cases where people tried to refuse the property, the IRS took the position that they had received the property and then made a (taxable) gift or an estate tax transfer to the next person in line. Under the old law, a key fact in determining whether there was a valid refusal (called a "disclaimer"), which, in turn, would avoid gift and estate taxes, depended in part on the effectiveness and timeliness of the disclaimer under the appropriate state law. However, because state laws varied, there was no uniform rule that applied.

What are the guidelines under the new law?

The 1981 law has provided new guidelines to achieve uniformity of result. Now a disclaimer will be effective for federal estate and gift tax purposes if it is made in writing within nine months of the time the person refusing the property interest is entitled to receive it (or, in appropriate cases, within nine months of the date the individual refusing the bequest reaches age twenty-one). State law will be applicable to determine the identity of the transferee but will no longer be applicable to determine what is a valid disclaimer. The written statement must be sent either to the transferor (if a gift is being disclaimed), to the executor of the estate (to disclaim a bequest under a will), or, where appropriate, to the person currently holding legal title to the property. The disclaiming individual also can't accept any of the benefits of the property. The disclaimer must be irrevocable, with no strings attached.

The new provision is effective for transfers after December 31, 1981.

For example, on January 1, 1981, Adam dies and provides a trust in his will. The income from the trust is left to Abel, and on the death of Abel, the principal is to be paid to Abel, Jr., or Abel, Jr.'s children.

At that time, Abel, Jr., is twenty-five years old. Abel, Jr., therefore has 9 months, until October 1, 1981, to send a written disclaimer to his father's executor stating his refusal to accept the interest in the trust. If he does, the disclaimer will not have any estate or gift tax consequences. If he delays past that date, for tax purposes he will be treated as having received the interest and then made a taxable gift of it.

If Abel, Jr., is twenty years old on January 1, 1981, and will not be twenty-one until March 15, 1981, he can wait 9 months after his 21st birthday, until December 15, 1981, to make the written disclaimer.

Repeal of Orphans' Deduction

Prior to the new law, an estate tax deduction was allowed from a parent's gross estate if the parent left one or more children under age twenty-one and the children became orphans at the parent's death. That provision is repealed for people dying after 1981.

Generation Skipping

Suppose Janet Hunt puts $1 million of property (cash and dividend paying stock) into a trust and provides for the income from the trust (interest and dividends) to be paid to her daughter, Betty. On Betty's death, she wants the principal paid to her grandson, Charlie.

Under the old law, when Betty died, her executor would not have had to include any part of the trust as part of her estate. The reason for this was that Betty's income interest would have ended when she died and this interest was all she had. She had no rights in the trust property itself.

Therefore, even though Betty got to enjoy the benefits of the trust property, the transfer of the property from Betty to Charlie didn't trigger any estate taxes.

In general, the estate tax is a generational tax, imposed on the transfer of property from one generation to the next. Here, because of the way the trust was set up, the estate tax "skipped a generation."

The law imposes a special tax on generation-skipping transfers under trusts or similar arrangements. This law requires a tax, measured by the amount of property transferred, to be paid by the trust beneficiary who is in the skipped generation. (In this case, it's Betty.)

When this law was first enacted in 1976, it contained a "transitional rule" that exempted from the generation-skipping tax those wills and trusts already in existence on June 11, 1976, if (1) the will or trust was not amended after that date to create or increase the amount of a generation-skipping transfer and (2) the creator of the will or trust died before January 1, 1982.

Under the new law, this date (January 1, 1982), contained in the present transitional rule, is extended one additional year to January 1, 1983.

Strategy Tip

If you have a will that created a generation-skipping trust prior to June 11, 1976, refrain from amending the generation-skipping transfer provision prior to January 1, 1982.

Special Use Valuation

For estate tax purposes, all of the property in your estate, including your real property (i.e., land, houses, buildings), is taxed at its fair market value. The estate tax law provides an exception for family farms and real property that is used in a family business. At the election of the estate, that kind of property may be valued at its "special use value," an amount that can be substantially less than its fair market value. The purpose of the special use valuation rules is to permit continuation of family ownership of farms and other businesses that might otherwise have to be sold to pay estate taxes.

What are the qualifications for special use valuation?

In order to make sure that this exception to the general estate tax valuation rules is limited to these situations (protecting the family farm or business), the special use valuation rules had many qualifications. Some of these were that the person whose estate was claiming the special treatment had to "materially participate" in the operation of the farm/business for a number of years prior to death; that after death the property had to remain in the family and be used for the special use (i.e., farm/business) for fifteen years or else the tax break would have to be paid back. In addition, the estate tax savings could in no event exceed $500,000.

The new law has made changes in all of these areas. First of all, the $500,000 is increased to $750,000 (Table 16).

Table 16
MAXIMUM BENEFIT FROM SPECIAL USE VALUATION

For Persons Dying in	Allowable Maximum Reduction
1981	$600,000
1982	700,000
1983 and later	750,000

The new law also liberalizes the special use valuation method by

- permitting the required business use of the property prior to the death of the taxpayer to have been conducted by a family member as well as the taxpayer. This change is retroactive to January 1, 1977.
- permitting the "material participation" test to be met in the case of a disabled or retired person before the beginning of his disability or retirement; and that surviving spouses, minor and disabled heirs, and full-time students meet the requirements by engaging in management decisions rather than day-to-day operations of the business.
- permitting certain postdeath exchanges of business property and involuntary sales to occur

83

without requiring a recalculation of the special valuation benefit. This change is effective for exchanges after 1981.

- permitting election for special use valuation to be made on a late-filed estate tax return as long as it is the first return filed.
- permitting special use valuation to be based on crop share rentals when there are no comparable cash rental standards.
- expanding the category of qualified heirs to include lineal descendants of the taxpayer's surviving spouse and of his parents.
- permitting qualified heirs to purchase property without jeopardizing the election for special use valuation.
- reducing from fifteen to ten years the period in which the tax saving obtained from special use valuation can be "recaptured" if the heir disposes of the property or stops its qualified use.
- introducing a two-year grace period after the death of the taxpayer during which failure by the heir to commence qualified use does not trigger recapture.
- permitting an increase in tax cost (for sale or other purposes) if a recapture tax is imposed.
- permitting woodlands property with standing timber to be qualify for special use valuation.

Part Two

Tax Changes for Business

9

The Corporation

If the changes in the new law affecting individuals are extensive and far reaching, the changes affecting businesses are by comparison nothing short of revolutionary. These changes and the tax savings opportunities they provide are essential to understand in order to make the right tax decisions for your business over the next several years.

Corporate Tax Rate Cuts

The income tax rates for corporations, unlike those for individuals, have only five steps. The maximum tax rate is 46 per cent. Prior to the new law, corporations paid tax according to the rate schedule as shown in Table 17.

The new law reduces the tax rate on taxable corporate income below $50,000, which helps small businesses, but retains the same rates (and the same 46 per cent maximum rate) for larger corporations.

Under the new law, corporations with taxable incomes of less than $25,000 will have their taxes reduced from 17 per cent to 15 per cent; the rate applied to corporations with taxable incomes of between $25,000 and $50,000 will go down from 20 per cent to 18 per cent. These reductions will be phased in two years as shown in Table 18.

Table 17
CORPORATE RATES UNDER PRIOR LAW

Taxable income	Rate
Less than $25,000	17
25,000–50,000	20
50,000–75,000	30
75,000–100,000	40
Over 100,000	46

Table 18
CORPORATE TAX REDUCTIONS UNDER THE NEW LAW

	Taxable Income	Rate
1982	Less than 25,000	16
	25,000–50,000	19
1983 and beyond	Less than 25,000	15
	25,000–50,000	18

Strategy Tip

Small corporations with less than $50,000 in taxable income should seek, if possible, to postpone the receipt of income from year-end 1981 to 1982 and again from year end 1982 to 1983. By doing this, they can shift income to years in which the lower rates will be effective. While the saving here may only be a minimal 1 percent, if the postponement is just for a few days, this savings will more than offset the loss of the use of the money.

Corporate Estimated Taxes

Under the old law, a corporation whose taxable income exceeded $1 million in any of the three preceding taxable years was required to keep its tax payments current by paying an estimated tax (in quarterly intervals over the year) of an amount equal to at least 60 percent of its current year's tax liability regardless of what it owed the year before. If it failed to do this, it was subject to a penalty.

The new law increases the 60 percent requirement to 80 percent, to be phased in over a three-year period (Table 19):

Table 19
INCREASE IN ESTIMATED TAX REQUIREMENTS

Year	Percentage
1982	65
1983	75
1984	80

As a result, the new law places a greater premium on careful calculation of current tax liability and cash management by a large corporation throughout the tax year.

10
Business Expenses

Corporate Charitable Contributions

The new law increases the amount of deductible contributions that corporations can make to charity. Beginning in 1982, the limit goes from 5 percent to 10 percent of taxable income.

Strategy Tip

A corporation planning to make charitable contributions equal to or near the 5 percent of taxable-income limit should postpone them until 1982 to ensure that they will be deductible.

Employee Gifts and Awards

Present law generally disallows business deductions for gifts to individuals in excess of $25. There is an exception, however, for items costing $100 or less that are awarded to an employee in recognition of length of service or for safety achievement.

The new law both increases the deductible amount of employee awards and expands the purposes for which they may be given. Employee awards can now be made for length of service, productivity, or safety achievement. And the new ceiling on these awards is increased from $100 to $400 per item.

In addition, the new law allows a deduction for employee awards made as part of a permanent written company plan or program. The only restrictions are that (1) the plan is not biased as to eligibility or benefits in favor of the corporate officers, shareholders or the more highly paid employees and that (2) the *average* cost of all of the awards under the plan during the year does not exceed $400 and cost of any single item does not exceed $1,600.

This amendment is effective for any taxable year ending after August 13, 1981.

Targeted Jobs Credit

Under the prior law, if you ran a business, you could claim a tax credit for certain wages you paid to any employees you hired from one or more of seven targeted economically disadvantaged groups. In general, the credit was equal to 50 percent of the first $6,000 you paid the employee in the first year of employment and 25 percent of the first $6,000 you paid during the employee's second year. The credit, however, could not exceed 30 percent of the total wages you paid to *all* your employees.

This credit, known as the "targeted jobs credit," was to expire on January 1, 1982. The new law extends it for one additional year and covers the employees you hire who begin work before January 1, 1983.

The new law also repeals the 30 percent limitation. Thus, the credit is computed without reference to the wages paid to nontargeted employees.

The new law makes the following additional modifications to the credit as well:

- Recipients of Aid to Families with Dependent Children (AFDC) and Work Incentive Program (WIN) registrants are added as a targeted group. The old WIN credit is merged into the targeted job credit.
- Eligible cooperative education students are limited to those who are economically disadvantaged.
- The age limitation for Vietnam veterans (age thirty-five) is eliminated.
- Laid-off public service employees funded by Comprehensive Employment and Training Act CETA are added as a targeted group.
- Certifications issued or requested after the individual begins work are invalid. Certifications

are to be performed by state employment security agencies.

- The credit is denied for rehired employees.
- The credit is denied for hiring relatives of the employers.

Tax Credit for Research and Experimentation

Prior to the new law, you could elect to take a current deduction for qualified research or experimental expenditures you incurred in connection with your trade or business, or you could amortize the research costs and spread out the deduction over a period of five years or more. These rules applied both to the costs of the research conducted by you and, in general, to the expenses you paid for research conducted on your behalf by a research firm or university. The IRS defines qualifying research expenditures as "research and development costs in the experimental or laboratory sense."

The new law now provides a special 25 percent tax credit for more limited class research and experimental expenditures that you incur after June 30, 1981, and before 1986. This credit is not automatic. You must elect it.

Under the new law, research expenditures qualifying for the new credit consist of (1) "in-house" expenditures for research wages and supplies, plus certain lease or other charges for research use of computers, laboratory equipment, and so on, (2) 65 percent of amounts paid (e.g., to a research firm or university) for contract research, and (3) 65 percent of corporate grants for basic research to be performed by universities or research corporations or to funds organized to make basic research grants to universities.

The new credit cannot be claimed for the costs of research conducted outside the United States, research in the social sciences or humanities, or research funded by a grant or contract.

How do you calculate the new credit?

The credit is only for incremental research costs and applies only to the extent that your current year expenditures exceed the average amount of research expenditures you had in a base period (generally, the preceding three years). The calculation involves several steps.

Because the new credit is effective for expenditures paid or incurred after June 30, 1981 (which comes in the middle of many businesses' tax years), there is a special rule for computing base period expenditures for the first year in which the new credit can be used. This rule is only applicable if that first tax year ends in 1981 or 1982. Under this special rule, the taxpayer's base period expenditures equal the total qualified research expenditures for the preceding taxable year multiplied by the following fraction:

$$\frac{\text{Number of months between June 30, 1981 and end of tax year ending after that date}}{\text{Number of months in the entire year}}$$

The above rule can be illustrated by the following situation: suppose you are a calendar-year taxpayer with research expenditures as shown in Table 20.

Table 20
HYPOTHETICAL RESEARCH EXPENDITURES

Year	Amount
1980	$100,000
1981	130,000
1/1/81–6/30/81	60,000
7/1/81–12/31/81	70,000
1982	150,000

For purposes of computing your 1981 credit, the base period amount would equal $100,000 times the fraction $^6/_{12}$, or $50,000. Therefore, your 25 percent credit for 1981 would apply to the difference between

$70,000 and $50,000, and the 1981 credit would be $5,000 (20,000 × 25 percent). For 1982, the credit would apply to the difference between your 1982 expenses of $150,000 and $115,000. For 1982 purposes, the $115,000 base period is figured by averaging ($100,000) and your 1981 expenses ($130,000). The 1982 credit would therefore be $8,750 ($30,000 × 25 percent).

In any event, under the new law, the base period research expenditures cannot be less than 50 percent of qualified research expenditures for the current year.

The 50 percent limitation rule can be illustrated by the following situation:

You organize a calendar year business on January 1, 1983, and make qualified research expenditures of $100,000 for 1983 and $260,000 for 1984. Since you are a new business for base period purposes, you are considered to have expenses of zero for pre-1983 years (the average of 1980 [zero], 1981 [zero], and 1982 [zero], or zero). However, because of the 50 percent limitation, your average base period expenditures are deemed to be no less than 50 percent of your current year expenditures ($100,000), or $50,000. Accordingly, the amount of expenditures eligible for the 1983 credit is $50,000, and the amount of your credit for 1983 is $12,500 ($50,000 × 25 percent).

The 1984 credit is similarly computed as follows: the base period is average for 1981 (zero), 1982 (zero), and 1983 ($100,000), or $33,333. However, because of the 50 percent limitation, your average base period expenditures are deemed to be no less than 50 percent of your current year expenditures ($130,000). Accordingly, the amount of expenditures eligible for the 1984 credit is $130,000, and the amount of your credit for 1984 is $32,500 ($130,000 × 25 percent).

Since the new law benefits only research paid "in carrying on a trade or business," the credit is not available if you pay for research as part of a hobby or in lending funds to someone who conducts the research. It is also not available if you underwrite research in the expectation of selling it for a royalty. The law does not recognize passive activities such as investing for royalties as "carrying on a trade or business."

Strategy Tip

The "trade or business" requirements will make it difficult for tax shelters to organize investments that can take advantage of the research credit. You should therefore look carefully at any shelter that promises to pass the research credit on to its investors.

Moreover, for each year, you should work out the computations for the new credit and the old deduction to determine which gives you a better deal. For some people, the application of the limitations on computing the credit (see below) may make the deductions more advantageous. If you have no tax liability for the year because of losses, the deduction may make better sense because the deduction will increase the loss available to be carried back or forward to another tax year.

Corporate Contributions of Newly Manufactured Equipment to Universities for Research

If a corporation makes a charitable contribution of its inventory property to a charity, its deduction for the gift is limited to the amount of its cost in the property. The corporation doesn't get a deduction equal to the property's current value. There is an exception for corporate contributions of certain property for use in the case of the needy, the ill, or infants. In that case, it can deduct the cost plus 50 percent of any appreciation (but not more than twice the cost). The appreciation is the difference between the cost and the property's current value.

The new law extends this rule (a deduction for cost plus 50 percent of any appreciation but not to exceed twice the cost) for corporate contributions of new

94

scientific equipment or apparatus that they manufacture and then give to a university for research in the United States in the physical or biological sciences. Without this special provision, such charitable gifts would produce only a "cost" deduction.

For example, suppose a corporation donates scientific equipment that it manufactures at a cost of $1,000 to a university. At the time of the gift, the equipment has a retail value of $4,000. The corporation is entitled to a deduction of $2,000 ($1,000 plus $1,500, or $2,500, but limited to $2 \times \$1,000$).

To qualify for the increased deduction, the contribution must be made within two years of manufacture; the property must be new property (not used property) in the university's hands, and the university may not acquire the property with the intent to sell or transfer it to another.

The new law is effective for contributions made after August 13, 1981.

Allocation of Research Expenditures to Domestic Income

A corporation operating both in the United States and abroad must allocate its research and experimentation costs between its U.S. operations and its foreign operations. To the extent the expenditures are allocated to its foreign operations and are charged against foreign-source income, the result is to reduce the company's available tax credit for foreign taxes, as allowed in another part of the law.

The new law provides that for two years corporate taxpayers with operations here and abroad must allocate all research expenses paid in activities conducted in the United States to U.S.-source income. This new rule will thus have the effect of maximizing the available foreign tax credit.

11
Business Investment

Some of the most far reaching and dramatic changes in the new law involve the expanded benefits for investments in business assets. The new law has introduced a new system for the cost recovery of business assets, known as the Accelerated Cost Recovery System (ACRS), replacing prior depreciation rules (although the old rules will continue to apply to assets acquired and placed in service before 1981). ACRS will cover all assets acquired and placed in service in 1981 and subsequent years. Under ACRS, business will be entitled to much more rapid tax write-offs for their investments without regard, as under prior law, to how long the assets are expected to be in service.

In this chapter, we will look at exactly how these new rules operate and how they are different from the depreciation rules for pre-1981 assets. We will also explain and review the other modifications and changes in the new law involving business investments, such as the investment tax credit, recapture rules, low-income housing, the minimum tax on preference income, and the new rules for leveraged leasing transactions.

Accelerated Cost Recovery System

The new law has substantially increased the annual deductions attributable to your business assets. The full import of these changes, however, is only fully understandable when we compare them to the prior law's depreciation rules.

How did depreciation work under prior law?

Under the old law, when you bought an asset and placed it in service in your business (a new machine, for example), the tax laws required that you spread the cost of the asset over its useful life in your business (say, ten years). The law did not permit you to deduct the entire cost of an asset in any single year. Thus, if the machine cost $45,000 and would have to be replaced after ten years (and if it would have no significant salvage value at the end of the period), you could, for example, deduct $4,500 each year for ten years. At the end of the ten-year period, the cost of the machine would be totally deducted or, in tax language, "recovered." The ten-year period is called the asset's "useful life" or "recovery period."

This annual deduction is called "depreciation." Under the old law, depreciation could be computed as in the above example, where the cost of the property was evenly spread over the ten-year period, the "straight-line" method, or it could be computed in accordance with various so called accelerated methods. For example, if double declining balance depreciation, one of the accelerated methods, was used for the above $45,000 asset, the depreciation deductions over its ten-year useful life would be as shown in Table 21.

Other accelerated methods were acceptable, too, producing a different schedule of deductions for the

Table 21
$45,000 MACHINE DEPRECIATED UNDER THE
DOUBLE DECLINING BALANCE METHOD

Year	Amount of Deduction
1	$9,000.00
2	7,200.00
3	5,760.00
4	4,608.00
5	3,686.40
6	2,949.12
7	2,949.12
8	2,949.12
9	2,949.12
10	2,949.12

asset. Under all of the accelerated methods, you were able to claim higher deductions in the early years than those available under the straight line method. But even when accelerated depreciation was permitted, the computation of the annual deduction under the old law was always tied to the asset's projected useful life in the taxpayer's business.

How does the asset's useful life affect the size of the depreciation deduction?

The shorter the useful life of an asset, the larger your annual depreciation deduction will be. In the above example, if your machine had a useful life of five years rather than ten, under the first depreciation calculation (straight-line), your yearly depreciation deduction would be $9,000 not $4,500. There would be similar benefits under the accelerated methods.

How did you know what an asset's useful life was under the old law?

Determining an asset's useful life for depreciation purposes under the old law was generally based on the Asset Depreciation Range (ADR) system. Under published Treasury guidelines, assets were grouped into about a hundred classes, with a useful life assigned to each class. That guideline life was then subject to a 20 percent tolerance range (longer or shorter). For example, an asset with a six-year ADR life could be depreciated over five, six, or seven years, at the taxpayer's option.

The ADR class lives were based on and roughly approximated the actual physical lives of the assets in the taxpayer's business. Thus, for example, business automobiles and taxis had a three-year guideline life, agricultural equipment had a ten-year life, printing and publishing machinery had an eleven-year life, and buildings (factories, banks, hotels, office buildings, etc.) had anywhere from a forty- to sixty-year guideline life, depending on the type of structure.

If a business computed the useful lives of its assets based on the ADR guidelines, it could be sure that they would not be challenged on audit by the IRS. It was always possible for a business to use its own estimate for determining the useful lives of its asset rather than the ADR system, but to do so, it would have to stand ready to prove that the useful life of the asset was an accurate one.

How is the Accelerated Cost Recovery System (ACRS) different?

The 1981 law makes major changes in the basic concept of useful life. Under the new law, business assets bought or placed in service after 1980 are now assigned to *four* broad categories (rather than 100), and their cost is recovered, over three, five, ten, or fifteen years, depending on the type of property involved and the category in which it belongs. Strikingly, these new recovery periods are unrelated to, and substantially shorter than, the assets' actual useful lives. That means that in most cases the actual life of the asset will be much longer than the period over which it can now be written off. These four new recovery periods apply to all depreciable property, both new and used.

The impact of the rules, which are known as the Accelerated Cost Recovery System or ACRS (and sometimes as "10-5-3") is to increase substantially the annual deductions attributable to depreciable assets that you can claim as a business taxpayer. By shortening the useful lives of all business assets, the new law will provide major tax savings for business. Proponents of the new rules hope that the tax savings will be used for investment in new plant and equipment and will, in turn, result in increased productivity and revenues.

What property is assigned to each category?

Under the new law, property eligible to be written off over three years includes car, light duty trucks, research and experimentation equipment, and certain other short-lived property. Most other tangible depreciable property (except buildings) is in the five-year class (such as machinery). The ten-year class includes "theme" park structures, railroad tank cars, and most public utility property. The fifteen-year category is for buildings and certain long-lived public utility property.

Are there optional longer recovery periods you can use?

Yes. To provide flexibility under the new system, (e.g., if your large write-offs under ACRS will provide deductions in excess of the amount you can use to offset income), you can elect to use an optional longer recovery period. There is an optional thirty-five- or forty-five-year period for property in the fifteen-year class; a thirty-five- or twenty-five-year period for property in the ten-year class; a twenty-five- or twelve-year period for property in the five-year class; and a twelve- or five-year optional period for property in the three-year class.

Strategy Tip

If you choose an optional recovery period, be aware that all of your property in that class must be depreciated on the same basis. Moreover, your choice, once elected, can only be revoked with the IRS's consent. On the other hand, the choice is not binding on property in other classes or property in the same class that is placed in service in another tax year. There is also a special rule for fifteen-year real property, for which you are allowed to elect a longer recovery period on a property-by-property basis.

How are the annual deductions on property within each category figured under ACRS?

Under ACRS, the percentage of the cost of an asset that can be deducted each year is not uniform but approximates one of the accelerated depreciation methods available under the old law. The following tables (Tables 22–24) show what percentage of your cost of the property in each new class you can deduct each year.

You may note that the first year's write-off in tables 23–25 is smaller than what you get in the second year and sometimes in subsequent years, too. This reflects use of the so-called half-year convention, which gives you credit for a half year of use in the first year. For administrative convenience, Tables 23–25 simply assume that you placed all assets in service on the first day of the second half of the year without regard to exactly when during the year you actually placed them in service in your business.

As of this date, no tables have been provided for the recovery percentages applicable to fifteen-year real property. In the near future, the IRS is expected to publish such tables. The tables will use the 175 percent declining balance method of depreciation and will not use the half-year convention.

The new ACRS rules do not replace the depreciation methods available under the prior law that were not based on useful life (e.g., the income forecast method or the unit of production method) even for assets acquired and used later than 1981.

What about assets used in your business before 1981?

As we noted earlier, the new ACRS rules do not apply to business assets you had in service prior to 1981. They only apply to assets placed in service in 1981 and thereafter. Pre-1981 assets will continue to be depreciated under the old rules. If you use a fiscal-year accounting system, the new rules apply only to assets placed in service in 1981 and thereafter. A fiscal-year taxpayer may therefore wind up having to use both the old and the new rules for new assets bought in its fiscal year 1981.

Table 22
COST RECOVERY PERCENTAGES
(1981-1984)

For property placed in service during 1981-1984, the applicable percentage for the class of property is:

Year	3 year	5 year	10 year	15-year public utility
1	25	15	8	5
2	38	22	14	10
3	37	21	12	9
4		21	10	8
5		21	10	7
6............			10	7
7............			9	6
8............			9	6
9............			9	6
10............			9	6
11............				6
12............				6
13............				6
14............				6
15............				6

Table 23
COST RECOVERY PERCENTAGES
(1985)

. For property placed in service in 1985, the applicable percentage for the class of property is:

Year	3 year	5 year	10 year	15-year public utility
1	29	18	9	6
2	47	33	19	12
3	24	25	16	12
4		16	14	11
5		8	12	10
6..........................			10	9
7..........................			8	8
8..........................			6	7
9..........................			4	6
10..........................			2	5
11..........................				4
12..........................				4
13..........................				3
14..........................				2
15..........................				1

Table 24
COST RECOVERY PERCENTAGES
(1986)

For property placed in service in 1986, the applicable percentage for the class of property is:

Year	3 year	5 year	10 year	15-year public utility
1	33	20	10	7
2	45	32	18	12
3	22	24	16	12
4		16	14	11
5		8	12	10
6			10	9
7			8	8
8			6	7
9			4	6
10			2	5
11				4
12				3
13				3
14				2
15				1

How these new rules operate is illustrated in the following example. Suppose the Williamson Dairy Co. purchases during 1981 a new milk truck for $18,000 and new office equipment (desks and typewriters) for $20,000. The truck is three-year ACRS property; the office equipment is five-year ACRS property. For 1981–1985 (the full recovery periods for these assets), the dairy's ACRS deductions will be as shown in Table 25.

Table 25
WILLIAMSON DAIRY–ACRS DEDUCTIONS (1981–1985)

	Truck	Office Equipment
Cost	$18,000	$20,000
1981	$4,500 (25%)	$3,000 (15%)
1982	6,840 (38%)	4,400 (22%)
1983	6,660 (37%)	4,200 (21%)
1984	—	4,200 (21%)
1985	—	4,200 (21%)

How these deductions compare with depreciation write-offs under prior law can be seen if we assume that our taxpayer, the Williamson Dairy, in addition to its milk truck purchases, also buys two new milking machines, each at a cost of $100,000. Suppose that the first machine was bought by the dairy in December 1980 and the second in February 1981. Under the new law, the machine acquired in February 1981 is eligible to be written off under ACRS; however, the machine purchased in December 1980 is not. It must be depreciated under the prior law.

Under ACRS, the February milking machine will be written off as five-year property. The December milking machine, however, must be depreciated over its eight-year ADR life. Table 26 demonstrates the smaller annual deductions that the dairy will get from its slower write-off of the machine purchased in December.

Table 26
WILLIAMSON DAIRY MILKING MACHINES—
COMPARISON OF ADR DEPRECIATION AND ACRS

	Depreciation	ACRS
	Milking Machine (December 1980)	Milking Machine (February 1981)
Cost	$100,000	$100,000
1981	$12,500.00	$15,000
1982	21,875.00	22,000
1983	16,406.25	21,000
1984	12,054.69	21,000
1985	9,291.02	21,000
1986	6,968.26	—
1987	5,226.20	—
1988	3,919.65	—

What are the "anti-churning" provisions?

Because of the more favorable tax treatment for business assets under ACRS, the new law contains specific provisions that bar you from "churning" your depreciation accounts either for real or personal business assets to bring them within the new ACRS rules. Thus, ACRS is specifically designated as inapplicable to depreciable personal property acquired during or after 1981, 1985, or 1986 if the property was previously owned or used by you or a related person, like your spouse. The new law also bars property you acquired after 1981, 1985, or 1986 through a tax-free exchange or a sale and lease-back transaction from coming under the new rules.

Similarly, ACRS is specifically inapplicable to depreciable buildings and other real property acquired after 1981, 1985, or 1986 in a sale and lease-back, tax-free exchange, or similar transaction or from a related person. By these prohibitions the law prevents you from bringing pre-1981 property within ACRS, or from utilizing the more favorable recovery percentages available after 1984 or 1985 for used property placed in service before 1985 or 1986.

Other antichurning rules prevent ACRS from applying to pre-1981-, 1985-, or 1986-owned personal or real business property that you transferred after 1981, 1985, or 1986 to a corporation or a partnership in a nontaxable transaction. As a result, you can't take advantage of the new faster write-offs by changing your business from a proprietorship to corporate or partnership form and then continuing business as usual.

What happens when you sell property on which you have claimed ACRS deductions?

If you sell property on which you have claimed ACRS deductions, your previously claimed ACRS deductions will be "recaptured," that is, the gain from the sale will be taxed as ordinary income to the extent of your prior ACRS deductions. This rule applies to all types of personal ACRS property as well as "theme" park structures, single-purpose agricultural and horticultural structures, and facilities used for the storage of petroleum and its primary products. It does not apply to

- Fifteen-year real estate that is residential rental property
- Fifteen-year real estate that is outside the United States
- Fifteen-year real estate for which a straight-line election is made
- Fifteen-year real estate that is subsidized low-income housing

Are there special rules that apply to the depreciation of buildings?

Under the new law, virtually all buildings are given a fifteen-year recovery period, although as we mentioned earlier, a taxpayer owning a depreciable building can elect to spread the deductions over a longer thirty-five- or forty-five-year period. Except for substantial improvements, which are treated as separate buildings, all components of a building are depreciated as an entire unit. Composite depreciation of individual components, such as plumbing, wiring, air conditioning systems, and so on, which is permitted under the old law, is not allowed under ACRS.

An improvement is treated as substantial (and thus its cost separately recoverable under ACRS) if, over two years, it constitutes at least 25 percent of the cost of the building (not taking into account depreciation or amortization deductions), and you add the improvement to the building at least three years after you first placed it in service.

What happens when you sell real estate on which you have claimed ACRS deductions?

As noted earlier, the IRS is expected to publish schedules showing the annual recovery percentages for real property investments in your business. These schedules will permit an accelerated write-off over the fifteen-year recovery period.

Under the old law, where accelerated depreciation was claimed on real property investments and the property was then sold, the portion of your gain recaptured as ordinary income was limited to a portion of the depreciation claimed (i.e., the excess of accelerated over straight-line depreciation).

Under the new law, the rules involving recapture of depreciation are different for commercial and residential real estate. The new rules say that if you sell commercial real estate on which you have taken ACRS deductions over a fifteen-year period, *all* of your gain, up to the amount of the ACRS deductions you have claimed, is taxable as ordinary income. If there is any balance, it is taxed at capital gains rates.

On the other hand, if the building is written off over

its fifteen-year recovery period using the straight-line method, you can report *all* of your gain at capital gains rates. And this is true even where a portion of the building (e.g., a substantial improvement) is depreciated over an elective longer thirty-five- or forty-five-year life.

For *residential* real estate on which you claim (accelerated) ACRS deductions over a fifteen-year period, the tax bite on "recapture" is less. Your gain on the sale is only ordinary income to the extent that ACRS deductions exceed the recovery that would have been allowed if you used the straight-line method over a fifteen-year useful life. The balance is capital gain. And if you use the straight line method, all of your gain is capital gain.

Investment Tax Credit

The investment tax credit has been a part of the Internal Revenue Code on and off since 1962. Initially enacted to stimulate business investment in machinery and equipment, the credit entitles business taxpayers to a 10 percent credit against the cost of any new depreciable business property placed in service during the year.

What were the applicable rules before the new law?

Under the old law, you could claim the credit for any property with a useful life of seven years or more. The property had to be "tangible personal property" (like machinery or office equipment) or other tangible personal property used in manufacturing, production, extraction, transportation, communications, electrical energy, gas, water, or sewage-disposal services. Generally, no credit was allowed for depreciable real property (buildings and their "structural components"). There were other exclusions as well, such as business property used outside the United States or property used by federal, state, or local governments.

If the "useful life" of the qualifying property was less than seven years, you could still claim the credit for a portion of the cost. For example, if the property had a useful life of five to six years, two-thirds of the cost was eligible for the credit. If the useful life of the property was three to four years, one-third of the cost was eligible for the credit. No credit could be taken for property with a useful life under three years, however.

What if you sold the property after claiming the tax credit?

The law also provided "recapture rules" to deal with situations in which the credit was claimed and then the property was disposed of before the end of its claimed useful life. For example, if you claimed the full investment credit on property you stated had a ten-year life and sold it after five years, you would have to pay back to the IRS some of the prior credit you claimed. The amount of the recaptured credit was figured by determining how much of the credit you would originally have been entitled to if the actual life had been known. For example, in the above example, where the sale of the property occurred after five years, one-third of your credit would be recaptured. That meant that you would have to add that amount to your tax liability for the year of sale.

What other limits were there?

First, the total amount of credit that could be used in any one year was limited. You couldn't use the credit to offset more than your first $25,000 of tax due for the year plus a percentage (increased from 50 percent to 90 percent over the years 1978–1982) of the balance. In addition, used property was subject to a $100,000 limit. What that meant was you could take the investment credit only on $100,000 of used property each year. But there was a three-year carry-back and a seven-year carry-forward right that applied to any unused credit.

What property qualifies for the investment credit under the new law?

The new ACRS rules have required some modifications in the investment credit since the amount of the investment credit you were entitled to under the old law was based on the useful life of the asset involved. The new law bases the investment credit on the recovery period of the property as determined by the ACRS rules.

Under the new law, 100 percent of the cost of five- or ten-year property, or fifteen-year public utility property, qualifies for the 10 percent investment credit. For property in the three-year class, 60 percent of the cost of the property qualifies for the credit. There are various exceptions. For example, commuter highway vehicles, although not in the five-year class, are entitled to the entire 10 percent credit on their full cost. Likewise, railroad cars, whether used in the United States or in a foreign country, also qualify for the credit with the exception that if the property is owned by a party that is other than a U.S. railroad corporation, it can't be leased to foreign companies for more than twelve months out of any two-year period.

The following example shows how the investment credit works under the new rules. Suppose Farmer Jones buys a new pickup truck and thresher for his farm during 1981 and immediately begins to use them. Jones will be entitled to an investment credit on these new purchases, computed as in Table 27. Therefore, Jones can claim an investment credit of $11,080 for 1981. This credit will offset his tax liability for the

Table 27
INVESTMENT TAX CREDIT UNDER THE NEW LAW

Asset	Recovery Period	Cost	Applicable Percentage	Qualified Investment	Investment Tax Credit (10%)
Pickup truck	3 years	$ 18,000	60	$ 10,000	$ 1,080
Thresher	5 years	100,000	100	100,000	10,000

year, dollar for dollar. Thus, if his tax bill was otherwise $15,000 Jones would owe only $3,920.

Have the "recapture" rules been modified, too?

Yes. Although the old recapture rules continue to apply to investment credit property placed in service before 1981, the new law has also added new recapture rules for dispositions of investment credit property placed in service in 1981 and thereafter.

For three-year property, one-third of the credit will be recaptured for each year under three years the property is not in service in the business. For five-year, ten-year, and qualifying fifteen-year property, the credit is recaptured at a rate of 20 percent a year for each year under five years it is not in service. For example, if you buy a three-year investment credit asset for $10,000, claiming a $600 credit (10 percent × 60 percent of cost), and you then sell it after using it for only two years, one-third of the claimed credit, or $200, is recaptured. Likewise, if you sell five-year property after four years of use in your business and you had previously claimed an $800 investment tax credit on the property, $160 of the credit must be paid back in the year of sale. Table 28 illustrates this rule.

As under the old law, recapture events include a sale

Table 28
RECAPTURE OF INVESTMENT CREDIT

If you sell the property	Percentage of credit	
	3-Year Property	15-Year, 10-Year, and 5-Year Property
Within the first year it is placed in service	100%	100%
After 1 year	66⅔%	80%
After 2 years	33⅓%	60%
After 3 years	No recapture	40%
After 4 years	No recapture	20%
After 5 years	No recapture	No recapture

or other taxable disposition of the property to a personal use and use of the property in a foreign country. Likewise, no recapture still results from a transfer that occurs because of the death of the owner or the tax-free liquidation of a subsidiary or in a nontaxable reorganization. In addition, if you simply change the form of conducting your business (from a partnership to a corporation, for example), this change in form will not be treated as a recapture event as long as you continue to use the investment credit property in your business and you retain a substantial interest in the business.

What about used property and carry-forwards under the new law?

The new investment credit also expands the $100,000 limit previously applied to used property. Under the new law, $125,000 of used property can qualify for the investment credit. This amount increases to $150,000 in 1985. In addition, carry-forwards of unused investment credit have been increased to fifteen years over the previous seven-year limit.

Are there any new restrictions?

Yes. One qualification that didn't exist under prior law is a new "at-risk" restriction for investments in qualifying investment credit property. This means that if you buy investment credit property on time and give back a note for a portion of the purchase price, you must be at risk on the note in order to claim the credit for the purchased property. If you have no personal liability for repayment of the note (e.g., the lender has only a security interest in the property sold) and if the lender is a related person, the cost of the property you have invested in will not be considered at risk, and you will not be eligible to claim the investment tax credit on that property.

In general, the rules governing the determination

whether you are at risk are the same as those applicable in limiting losses under other existing provisions of the tax law. This new restriction is applicable to individuals, Subchapter S corporations and certain family or other small corporations. As with some other at-risk limitations in the tax law, real estate activities and certain kinds of leasing activities are given an exemption. In addition, if you have put up at least 20 percent of the cost of the property and the balance is borrowed from a bank, savings and loan association, credit union, insurance company, or other person or entity that is in the business of lending money, the at-risk rules will not apply. The at-risk rules also don't apply to borrowed funds used to buy "qualified energy property" if you put up at least 25 percent of the cost of the property on a recourse basis. Qualified energy property includes solar or wind equipment, recycling equipment, hydroelectric generating property, and so on.

Finally, in some cases, you can have a fluctuating amount at risk and additional credits on recaptured amounts. Ask your accountant about the new rules if this affects you.

Strategy Tip

Don't worry about making purchases of investment credit property late in the year. Even if you purchase the property and place it in service at the end of the year, you will be entitled to the full amount of the investment credit on your qualified investment for the year.

What about the tax credit for rehabilitation expenditures?

Under the new law, there is a new 15 percent investment tax credit that applies to the cost of rehabilitating buildings that are at least thirty years old; a new twenty percent investment credit that can be used for buildings over 40 years old; and a new 25 percent investment credit that may be claimed for costs of rehabilitating certified historic structures. The new credits have replaced the ten percent rehabilitation credit that existed under the prior law. (There is no investment tax credit for the cost of rehabilitating a building under thirty years old.)

These new tax credits for rehabilitation expenditures were intended to balance the substantial incentives created in the new law (through the new ACRS and investment tax credit provisions) for investments in *new* property. In other words, with taxpayers now being able to write off the costs of constructing new buildings over a fifteen-year period, businesses might well find it substantially more cost effective to tear down existing structures and build a lot of new commercial ones rather than to rehabilitate existing older buildings that frequently provide character and architectural diversity in the community.

The 15 percent and twenty percent investment tax credits adopted in the new law apply to nonresidential buildings only. On the other hand, the 25 percent investment tax credit applicable to certified historic structures may be used in the case of both residential and nonresidential properties.

You should know that under the new law, to the extent this new investment tax credit is claimed for a portion of the rehabilitation expenditures, that amount is not subject to depreciation. For example, suppose you spend $40,000 rehabilitating a forty-five-year-old building. The investment tax credit applicable to the rehabilitation expenditures will be $8,000. The amount of the rehabilitation expenditures eligible for depreciation will be $32,000.

What are substantial rehabilitation expenditures?

Since only qualified rehabilitation expenditures are eligible for the new rehabilitation tax credits, what counts as a rehabilitation expense is obviously of key importance.

First of all, there must be a "substantial" rehabilitation effort. Simple redecorating or repairs won't do. In this regard, the rehabilitation expenditures in the preceding two-year period must exceed either $5,000 or the taxpayer's "adjusted basis" (generally, cost less depreciation deductions) in the property, whichever is larger.

As under other laws, the cost of buying the building to be rehabilitated does not count, nor does the cost of completing construction on a building once it has been placed in service in your business. Moreover, the law considers that if more than 25 percent of the external walls of the building are replaced, you have engaged in new construction rather than rehabilitation, and the cost won't be considered eligible for the new investment tax credit. Enlarging a building is also not rehabilitation under the new law's standards. Look for regulations on this point.

Can a lessee claim the new rehabilitation expenditure tax credits?

If the rehabilitation is done by someone who is leasing the property, that person is eligible to claim the investment tax credit for the rehabilitation cost. There is one limitation: at the time rehabilitation is completed, the lease term must have at least fifteen years to run.

Do the qualified rehabilitation expenditures count as used property for purposes of the used property limitation? And are the rehabilitation credits subject to recapture?

The answer to the first question is no. The rehabilitation expenditures will be treated as new investment credit property, and the used property limits are therefore irrelevant. However, the rehabilitation expenditures *are* subject to the general investment credit recapture rules, as described earlier, which apply to fifteen-year ACRS property.

Expensing Privilege

Because of the new shortened recovery periods available under ACRS for the depreciation of business assets, the provision under the old law that permitted a "bonus" first-year depreciation deduction has been repealed. However, that provision, which was contained in Section 179 of the Internal Revenue Code, has been replaced with a *new* Section 179, and this new Section 179 provides an equally attractive tax deduction.

The new Section 179 now permits a taxpayer (other than a trust or an estate) to deduct ("expense") all in one year, the cost of certain qualified property, which is placed in service after 1981. In other words, you don't have to recover it over a period of years. For 1982 and 1983, the taxpayer can elect under this provision to deduct currently up to $5,000 of qualifying property. For 1984 and 1985, the $5,000 limit is increased to $7,500. For 1986 and thereafter, the dollar limit is again increased to $10,000 of qualified property.

In general, "qualified property" is tangible personal property acquired by the taxpayer by purchase and used in a trade or business. The property must be eligible for the investment credit. To prevent multiple use of the new Section 179, special rules are provided for claiming the benefits of Section 179 by a controlled group of corporations and by partners and partnerships.

You should note that this provision is not automatic. You must elect to come within it. You should also note that the new Section 179 doesn't start until 1982, whereas the old Section 179 has been repealed as of 1981. Therefore, neither the old additional first-year bonus depreciation nor expensing under the new law is allowed for property placed in service in tax years beginning in 1981.

If the new Section 179 is used and the applicable property is later disposed of, the amount deducted will be treated as depreciation, and the depreciation recapture rules will apply.

How is the Section 179 election made?

The election to "expense" property under the new Section 179 is made on the tax return for the year in which the property is purchased. Once made, the election is irrevocable. If you later sell or otherwise dispose of the asset, the amount claimed under Section 179 is treated as depreciation and subject to the recapture rules that we have already described. Moreover, if the property is expensed under the new Section 179, no investment credit can be taken for that property.

Strategy Tip

Even though you are losing the investment credit, the tax benefits you will get from the immediate write-off of the asset will in almost every case be greater than the slower write-off of the investment credit.

Qualifying Section 179 property must be acquired by "purchase." For purposes of the new provision, the term *purchase* does not include property acquired from a related person (as defined in the tax laws) or property acquired from one member of a control group of corporations by another member of the group. In addition, for purposes of Section 179, there is no purchase if the tax cost of the property in the hands of the person acquiring it is determined in whole or in part by reference to the tax cost of the property in the hands of the person from whom it was acquired. Section 179 is therefore unavailable for property acquired in certain tax-free reorganizations. Finally, "purchase" excludes property acquired from an estate.

Low-Income Housing

Traditionally, a key component of real estate tax shelters has been the deduction for construction period interest and taxes. In 1976, the tax laws were changed to require you in most situations to spread the deduction of these costs over ten years rather than deduct them in the current year. Low-income housing was given a temporary break. It was to be exempt from the ten-year amortization requirement until 1982.

The new law has now made this exemption permanent. The result is that investors who build low-income housing projects can deduct costs of interest and taxes incurred during the construction phase of the project, while those who invest in other kinds of construction projects, like office buildings, are subject to the ten-year amortization rule.

Another pre-1981 provision in the tax law applicable to low-income housing permitted investors who bought older structures and then rehabilitated them and rented them to low-income families to write off the rehabilitation costs, up to $20,000 per apartment unit rehabilitated over an accelerated five-year period. Without this special provision, the period over which the rehabilitation costs were deductible would be anywhere from twenty to forty years. The new law increases the $20,000 limit to $40,000 per unit. However, to qualify for a $40,000 per unit write off, the new law requires the owners to sell the apartments to tenants who show home ownership responsibilities and limits the owners' profit on such sales to the tax deductions obtained from the investment. Thus, the sale price cannot reflect any market appreciation in the underlying real estate. The object is to permit low-income families to buy rehabilitated housing at prices they can afford. The tradeoff for the seller is a tax deduction, not a large profit on the real estate transaction.

Minimum Tax/Maximum Tax

The minimum tax is a 15 percent "add-on" tax that was enacted in 1969 when it became apparent that through the various exclusions, deductions, and credits permitted in the tax law, a sizeable number of taxpayers with substantial incomes (sometimes $1 million or more) were paying no tax. The minimum tax was intended to insure that *everyone* would pay some tax.

The tax is imposed only on so-called "preference items", that is, the amount of various enumerated tax benefits and deductions claimed on other parts of the tax return.

In computing the amount subject to the minimum tax, you deduct either $10,000 or one half of your regular tax liability for the year, whichever is larger. This eases the burden of the minimum tax on people whose preference items are relatively small or who are in fact paying regular income tax. Tax preference items also in the past have reduced the amount of your earned income that was subject to the 50 percent maximum tax.

How are the minimum and maximum tax preference items affected by the new law?

The new law changes these rules in several respects. First, in 1981 preference items will continue to reduce earned income eligible for the 50 percent maximum tax. After 1981, however, when the maximum rate on *all* income is 50 percent, this rule will no longer be necessary.

Second, one of the tax preference items listed in the tax law and subject to the minimum tax is the excess of any depreciation you took on leased personal property under any accelerated method, over the depreciation deduction you would have been entitled to if you had used the straight line method. Another tax preference item under the old law was for the excess of real property depreciation you claimed on an accelerated method over the same depreciation computed on the straight line method. The new law has amended these provision to conform to the new ACRS rules.

The new law substitutes as a tax preference item the excess of the ACRS deduction claimed for leased personal property over the straight line depreciation that would have been available for such property using a recovery period (Table 29).

In making the computation, any salvage value the property would have at the end of its life is disregarded. Also the half-year convention is used, an automatic rule that assumes that property placed in service during the course of the year is entitled to a half year's depreciation in its first year.

For example, suppose Paul Heller is a 20 percent partner in a business that leases computers. A new computer is purchased on January 1, 1982, for $100,000, which is eligible to be written off under the new ACRS rules as five-year property. In 1982, the partnership claims a $15,000 ACRS deduction for such property (Table 22) Under the straight-line method of depreciation and using an eight-year life, the 1982 allowance would have been $12,500. Therefore, the partnership has a 1982 tax preference item of $2,500 of which Paul's share is $500.

For depreciable buildings and other real property, the amount of the tax preference under the new law will be the excess of the ACRS deduction claimed for

Table 29
LEASED PERSONAL PROPERTY

Class of Property	Recovery Period
3-year property	5 years
5-year property	8 years
10-year property	15 years
15-public utility property	22 years

the year over the amount that would have been allowable, using the straight-line method and a fifteen-year recovery period.

Leveraged Leasing

As a general rule, depreciation deductions and investment tax credits may be claimed only by the owner of property. Where property is leased, it is generally the lessor/owner who is entitled to these tax benefits, not the lessee.

Why are leasing arrangements used?

Many companies in the steel, automobile, airline, and railroad industries are presently unable to absorb and use against their income the full benefit of their large depreciation deductions and investment tax credits. These are industries that are capital intensive, and so deductions and credits from these sources are significant. In recent years, however, many of the companies operating in these industries have not shown substantial profits.

In recent years, companies in these industries have begun to lease capital equipment rather than buy it, thereby permitting them to have and use the property without making a major capital investment. In addition, by leasing, they get to deduct the rent paid to the lessors as a business expense. These transactions have been beneficial from the lessor's standpoint, too, because they (frequently tax shelter limited partnerships) become entitled to the general depreciation and investment tax credit write-offs.

Some of the leases used in these transactions are "direct leases," that is, where the money used to purchase the asset that is leased to the company is from the lessors' own pocket. In other cases, however, the funds used to acquire the leased property by the lessors are borrowed. The latter leases are known as "leveraged leases."

How exactly does a leveraged lease transaction work?

In a typical leveraged lease transaction, the lessor will put up a percentage of the cost (usually about 20–40 percent) and will then borrow the balance, usually on a basis involving no personal liability (nonrecourse) from a bank or other financial institution. The loan will be secured by a mortgage on the purchased property. In addition, the lessor may give the lender (bank) as security for the loan an assignment of the lease and an assignment of the rental payments under the lease. The lessor, as the owner of the property, will then take tax deductions for depreciation and investment tax credits on the leased property.

In the past, the IRS permitted the tax benefits that flow from such arrangements to pass muster only if the transaction was economically sound and not simply a financing arrangement in which the lessor had no real interest in the underlying property.

How did you know if your transaction was economically sound for IRS purposes?

The IRS standards for measuring this were as follows:

- The lessor's minimum at-risk investment in the property was at least 20 percent of the property's cost.
- The lessor had a positive cash flow, and the leased transaction was profitable to the lessor independent of the tax benefits.
- At the end of the lease, if the lessee had an option to purchase the property, the option price had to be at market value.
- The lessee had not invested in the lease, that is, had not loaned any of the purchase price to the owner.
- The property must have had some useful life at the

end of the lease term and be commercially usable by a person other than the lessee.

How does the new law change the leveraged leasing rules?

The new law substantially liberalizes these requirements for determining the validity of a leveraged lease and creates a "safe harbor" which, if fully complied with by the lessor, will guarantee that the transactions will be characterized as a lease for tax purposes. Thus, the lessor will be entitled to claim the investment credit and the ACRS allowances.

Under the new law, all of the parties to the transaction must affirmatively elect to treat the lessor as the owner of the property. In addition, the lessor must be a corporation, a partnership of corporations, or a particular type of trust, the creator and beneficiaries of which are all corporations. Subchapter S corporations and personal holding companies cannot qualify under the new law, nor can individuals or partnerships. For the entire term of the lease and also at the time when the property is placed in service, the lessor must have directly invested 10 percent of the cost of the property. Finally, the length of the lease (including all extensions) can't be longer than 90 percent of the actual useful life of the property or 150 percent of the ADR class life (as measured under prior law. (See our earlier discussion in this Chapter.)

Only new property can come within this safe harbor. In addition, the property must, of course, be eligible under ACRS and the investment tax credit for these write-offs. The property must also be leased within three months after it is placed in service, so that it would have been considered new investment credit property if the lessee had acquired it directly and used it in its business.

If all of the above requirements are met, the IRS will automatically permit the transaction to be treated as a lease for purposes of assigning the right to the investment credit and the ACRS allowances. It is note-worthy that if at any time during the lease the lessee acquires the property, the safe harbor requirements are not met, and the lessee is treated as the owner of the property.

Strategy Tip

Be careful of the new at-risk rule that applies to the investment tax credit.

Why is this change so significant?

The key requirement that the IRS used under prior law to determine the validity of a lease transaction (i.e., the profitability test without regard to tax benefits) has been dropped under the new law. The minimum at-risk investment has also been cut in half from 20 percent to 10 percent of the cost of the property. Other factors that will no longer be taken into account by the IRS for determining whether the transaction constitutes a valid lease include the fact that the lessee, for state tax purposes, is treated as the nominal owner of the property because the lessee retains the title to the property and all obligations with respect to it, such as keeping the property in good repair and paying taxes on it.

These new provisions are generally viewed as an authorization for corporations that cannot use their tax benefits (because they're operating at a loss or for other reasons) essentially to sell the benefits to other high-bracket taxpayers through the lease mechanism.

The point of all of this is best illustrated in the following example.

Suppose the Celestial Airline Company, which has been only marginally profitable in recent years, buys a new $8 million airplane. The purchase immediately gives the carrier a $800,000 investment tax credit that it can't use because it doesn't have enough tax liability. But Acme Computers, a profitable computer company, can use the tax credit and therefore agrees to "lease" the airplane to Celestial. The parties therefore work out the following arrangement.

Acme will buy the airplane from Celestial, making a 10 percent ($800,000) down payment and giving the airline a $7.2 million note for the balance. The note has a five-year term at a market rate of interest. As the owner of the property, Acme can now claim the 10 percent investment tax credit against its income for the year ($800,000), as well as first-year depreciation on the airplane.

The payments on Acme's note will be the same as the rent it charges for the airplane, so no money will change hands. However, Acme will get an additional tax deduction for the interest on the note it is credited with paying to Celestial.

Celestial will be responsible under the lease for all insurance, maintenance, and other costs during the lease term, so Acme has no additional expenses. The lease further provides that at the end of five years Celestial can buy the plane for $1.

What mutual benefits flow from this arrangement?

From Acme's standpoint, it has gotten an $800,000 investment tax credit, five years of ACRS deductions on an $8 million asset, and five years of interest deductions on its $7.2 million loan to Celestial—all this at an $800,000 cost. As for Celestial, its sale of the airplane to Acme has resulted in its acquiring an $8 million asset for $7.2 million.

Under prior law, this transaction would not have passed muster because it met none of the IRS standards. Now the ground rules are different.

That is why many tax professionals are saying that the new provisions are a bonanza for troubled companies that could revolutionize corporate financing of capital assets.

12
The Small Corporation

The new law provides three significant reforms for small businesses. First, it liberalizes the requirements for a corporation to elect to be taxed under Subchapter S and avoid payment of the corporate tax. Second, it insulates small businesses from the threat of accumulated earnings tax liability. Third, it offers simplified inventory accounting rules for small businesses that can help save taxes in an inflationary economy.

Tax Option (Subchapter S) Corporations

As a result of tax legislation first enacted in 1958, certain corporations are entitled to file an election with the IRS that permits them to be exempt from the corporate income tax. The taxable income of these corporations is passed through to the shareholders and reported by the shareholders on their individual returns for the year in much the same way as the members of a partnership do. However, even though a Subchapter S corporation is not subject to the corporate income tax, it is a bona fide corporation for state law purposes, that is, it has limited liability, centralized management, and so on.

A Subchapter S election is particularly advantageous for a business just starting up. If it incurs losses, those losses can be "passed through" to the shareholders to shelter other income on their individual returns. However, when the business becomes profitable, the profits are taxable to the shareholders whether or not the corporation in fact distributes them. In those circumstances, the shareholders often revoke the Subchapter S election so that the corporation will revert to normal status. It will then be subject to tax on its own income, and the shareholders will be taxed only if they receive distributions.

Not all corporations are entitled to elect Subchapter S status. To make an election under Subchapter S, the law imposes severe restrictions on the number of shareholders, the type of shareholders of the corporation (only individuals, estates, and certain kinds of trusts), the corporation's affiliation with other corporations, and the type of income that the corporation earns.

What has the new law done to Subchapter S?

Under the 1981 law, some of the eligibility requirements of Subchapter S have been liberalized.

One of the requirements under prior law for electing Subchapter S status was that the corporation could have no more than fifteen shareholders. The 1981 law increases that number to twenty-five.

The law also liberalizes the rules applicable to Subchapter S shareholders that are trusts. Prior to the 1981 law, only certain trusts could become shareholders in a Subchapter S corporation. If a nonqualifying trust became a shareholder or if a qualifying trust remained a shareholder for longer than the rules allowed, the Subchapter S election would immediately terminate, and the corporation would be subject to the corporate tax for that tax year. Under the new law, a trust that is treated as owned by a person other than the creator of the trust can be an eligible Subchapter S shareholder.

In addition, the new law permits so-called qualified Subchapter S trusts to be shareholders in Subchapter S corporations without terminating the election. A qualified Subchapter S trust is a trust that owns stock in a Subchapter S corporation and that has only one income beneficiary at any one time. In addition, the income beneficiary must be a citizen or resident of the United States. All of the income of the Subchapter S trust must be distributed to the income beneficiary. However, during the term of the trust, the principal of the trust can be distributed to the income beneficiary. Where a Subchapter S trust intends to be a stockholder in a Subchapter S corporation, the beneficiary of the trust must file a special election that is irrevocable. The election under the new law may be made retroactive for up to sixty days.

The new law is effective for taxable years beginning after December 31, 1981.

Accumulated Earnings Credit

The law prevents a corporation from unreasonably accumulating its excess earnings and profits without paying dividends of those earning to its shareholders. It does this by imposing a special "accumulated earning tax" on any earnings that are accumulated beyond the reasonable needs of the business. If it were not for the accumulated earnings, the owners of a corporation could arrange to have their corporation retain all its earnings, have them taxed only at corporate rates (which at 46 percent may be lower than the highest rates that apply to individuals) and then sell the stock of the corporation paying only capital gains tax. The earnings of the company (which would be taxed to the shareholders at ordinary rates if paid out in dividends) will, because they were retained in the corporation, enhance the value of the stock. Therefore the owners could transform their ordinary income (dividends) into capital gain (sale of stock), which is taxed at a lower rate. In addition, even if the owners held the stock until their deaths and then gave the stock to their children, the dividend tax would still be avoided. Because the children would receive the stock as a bequest, the law would permit them, when they sold the stock, to treat as their gain only the difference between the sales price and the *value* of the stock when they received it, not the cost to the parent. This would result in major loss of tax revenues.

For example, suppose you start a corporation with $50,000. Over the next twenty years, it prospers and accumulates over $1 million in earnings without paying any dividends to you. Therefore, when you die, the stock is worth $1 million. You leave the stock to your children, who then sell it, two years later, for $1.2 million. If you had sold the stock prior to your death, your gain would be figured by subtracting your cost from the sales price. Therefore, if you had sold it for $1 million, your taxable gain would have been $950,000. In addition (unlike dividends), it would have been taxed as a capital gain. Assume, however that you leave the stock to your children and that they sell the stock. They will have only a $200,000 gain on the sale, the difference between the $1 million value of the stock at your death (their tax cost or "basis") and the sales price. The gain on the $950,000 appreciation during the period you held the stock, which represents accumulations of earnings, is extinguished.

In order to prevent (1) the transformation of ordinary income (dividends) into capital gain (which occurred in the example when the stock was sold by you, prior to death) and (2) the avoidance of tax altogether if you hold the property until your death, the law requires current distribution of dividends, or else an "accumulated earnings tax" will be imposed on the corporation.

The old law allowed corporations to claim a credit of $150,000 in computing their accumulated earnings tax base. This credit was allowed so some corporate earnings could be retained for the reasonable needs of the business.

The new law increases the accumulated earnings credit to $250,000 except for service corporations engaged in health, law, engineering, architecture, accounting, actuarial science, performing arts, and consulting, which are still subject to the old credit limit.

The new provision is effective for taxable years beginning after December 31, 1981.

Inventory Rules

The tax law has long permitted the use of inventory accounting for the computation of the taxable income of businesses engaged in selling. The inventory method of accounting eliminates the need to maintain records tracing individual purchases and sales on an item-by-item basis. Under inventory accounting, you measure your inventory as of the beginning and the end of the year. The difference between the two figures is the cost of goods sold. If you use an inventory method of accounting, you determine your profit by subtracting your cost of goods sold and other expenses from your gross sales proceeds.

One of the accepted methods of inventory accounting is the "last-in, first-out" or "LIFO" method. Under the LIFO method, you assume that you sell the most recently purchased goods first. LIFO is, therefore, a method of accounting that, during periods of inflation, results in the highest cost of goods sold being deducted from revenue. As a result, the LIFO method is an advantageous way to produce lower taxable income in a period of inflation when the cost of goods sold continues to increase.

There are two basic methods for determining LIFO inventories. The first method is based on actual quantities and costs. The second is the dollar-value method. Under dollar value, you measure your inventory on the basis of a pool of dollars. In general, the pool of dollars is actually measured in terms of the equivalent dollar value of the inventory in the year that you first used the dollar-value LIFO method.

Dollar-value LIFO is an advantageous method of computing LIFO inventories, but because of its inherent complexity, it is considered by some, especially small businessmen, as unworkable. The new law seeks to simplify the use of the dollar-value LIFO method for small businesses. Under the new law, businesses with average gross receipts of less than $2 million for the past three years (ending with the current year) may elect a single pool for purposes of dollar-value LIFO. In addition, businesses electing LIFO will have three years (beginning with the year of the election to LIFO) to take back into income inventory write-downs taken in prior years. In this way, the tax burden of switching to the more advantageous LIFO method will be eased.

Finally, the new law directs the IRS to simplify the dollar-value LIFO method by permitting all businesses to use published government price indexes to determine the value of inventories. Prior to the new law, the only businesses that were allowed to use such indexes were department stores.

The inventory changes are effective for taxable years beginning after December 31, 1981.

Strategy Tip

If you are considering a change to the LIFO method, you should generally postpone the conversion until your tax year beginning after December 31, 1981, or thereafter.

13
Tax Shelters

To understand fully the changes brought about by the new law, it is important to consider some basic facts about how a tax shelter works. In this chapter, we will look at tax shelters in general. We will then focus on what impact the new law has had on tax shelters and how these changes can affect you.

What is a Tax Shelter?

Though many different types of tax shelters exist, the common characteristic of them all is that they produce "tax losses" that are available as deductions not only against your share of taxable income from the tax shelter investment but also against your taxable income from other sources, such as from your business or profession. Through such investments, you can therefore "shelter" your regular income from tax.

Tax shelter investments produce such savings by three mechanisms. These are "deferral," "leverage," and "conversion." Not all tax shelters have all three features, but most have at least two.

"Deferral" is the ability to postpone tax liability into a later year. A general characteristic of a tax shelter investment is that it generates substantial tax losses, particularly in the early years of the investment, which you can use to reduce your tax liability on your unrelated income. The investment produces taxable income, if any, only in later years. Therefore, tax liability on your regular source of income is deferred until income resulting from the tax shelter is realized. The effect of deferral is very much like an interest-free loan from the IRS because you get the use of your tax dollars for the early years of your tax shelter investment.

A second element of many tax shelters involves the use of someone else's money (usually a bank or other financial institution's) to finance the shelter's investment activity and the tax deductions. This is called "leverage." Frequently, a tax shelter is set up so that you (or your partnership, through which you make the tax shelter investment) will borrow 80 percent or more of the purchase price of the investment.

From an economic standpoint, the more the investment activity can be financed with borrowed money, the less equity you have to put up to buy into the shelter. From a tax standpoint, moreover, you are allowed deductions (such as depreciation and the investment credit) not only on your equity contribution to the venture but also on the borrowed funds used to acquire the investment property. Through a minimal investment, therefore, it is possible to generate deductions that can substantially exceed your equity investment.

For example, assume you are a 10 percent partner in a tax shelter partnership (real estate, equipment leasing, etc.) that requires $1 million of capital. If you and your tax shelter partners invest $100,000 in cash (your share is $10,000) and you borrow $900,000 from a bank for the balance, for tax purposes you (and your partners) are treated as having put $1 million into the investment. It is that amount on which the deductions are calculated. Now suppose the shelter produces first-year deductions of $200,000, of which your share is $20,000. If you are in the 70 percent bracket, your tax shelter will reduce your taxes by $14,000 ($20,000 × 70 percent). In this case, your savings in the first year ($14,000) would be $4,000 more than the amount you originally invested ($10,000). These deductions would continue in subsequent years. The reason your investment produced such large deductions was because it was highly leveraged, that is, the deductions were financed using someone else's money.

In some cases, these benefits can be achieved where

you are not even personally liable for repayment of the borrowed money, that is, the lender can look for the repayment of the loan only to the property purchased with the borrowed funds. This is called "nonrecourse financing." Leveraging tax benefits with nonrecourse financing has been substantially tightened in recent years, however.

"Conversion," the third savings feature of many tax shelter investments, is the attempted transformation of ordinary income into capital gains, which is taxed at lower rates. What is sought is that at the time of the sale either of the investment assets (e.g., an apartment building) or of your partnership interest in the shelter, any gain is treated as capital gain, not ordinary income. If such gain is so treated, it involves a conversion of ordinary income into capital gain because the losses from the shelter that produced the tax savings were used to offset your income. Now you seek to make your gain from the shelter eligible for capital gains tax rates.

The ability to accomplish this goal has been somewhat limited by the recapture rules applicable to the sale of depreciable assets.

How are tax shelters marketed?

In order to sell tax shelter benefits to people who are not directly engaged in the activity, the most common investment vehicle is the limited partnership. The limited partnership form is usually chosen because it allows the immediate flow-through to the investor of the shelter's losses and also because it provides the investors with limited liability. Flow-through is available because partners, unlike shareholders of corporations, obtain an immediate deduction on their return for their proportionate share of the partnership tax losses. Also, by making the tax shelter investors limited partners, their financial risk, like that of shareholders in a corporation, is limited to their equity in the partnership.

How risky are tax shelter investments?

Tax shelter investments always present some risk. Some are substantially riskier than others. Any shelter you are considering investing in should be carefully and individually reviewed before you decide to invest.

The risks basically fall into two categories. First, there may be risk in the underlying transaction. As in all investments, you will therefore want to look closely at the economic strength of the underlying investment. This is important because though cash flow may not be your primary motivation, if the underlying transaction fails (e.g., the apartment building your tax shelter partnership owns is foreclosed, or the the cattle farming operation goes bankrupt because of unanticipated increases in grain prices), the tax shelter will also fail. When that happens, both the equity you have already put up and all of your future tax benefits will be lost. In addition, the very termination of the investment will usually result in unfavorable tax consequences, requiring you to pay back most or all of the prior deductions you had previously claimed (the deferred income—)and at ordinary income rather than capital gains rates.

A second level of risk you assume when you invest in a tax shelter is that even if the transaction is a success, the IRS may not accept the tax benefits you claimed as a result of your tax shelter participation. In some shelters, the promoters take positions for purposes of reporting the tax partnership's income that are highly questionable, indeed sometimes even reckless. These show up as rosy projections when you are buying an interest in the shelter. But at a later time they may be disallowed when your return (or the partnership's return) is audited. You may also be required to pay legal fees to defend the tax benefits you have claimed. Therefore, the risk of the possible loss of your tax benefits later on should be carefully studied.

Strategy Tip

Though tax shelters can save you money, they can also wind up costing you a fortune. Ask your lawyer or another tax professional to examine a potential shelter for you before you make the decision to go in.

What are the various kinds of tax shelters?

In the past, tax shelters have followed the specialized investment areas given favored treatment under the tax law such as depreciation, the investment tax credit, depletion, and the like. Among the more popular shelters are real estate investments (both in commercial and residential rental property), cattle farming, equipment leasing, and various entertainment shelters like motion pictures. Tax shelters have also been promoted for investments in professional sports franchises, lithographs, and others.

When do tax shelters make sense as an investment?

In the past, the marketing of interests in tax shelter ventures have generally been directed at taxpayers whose marginal tax rates were 50 percent or above. Promotional literature on tax shelter offerings usually advises potential investors that the primary benefit of the investment is the tax deductions generated in the early years of the investment. The prospect of a substantial economic return is normally of secondary importance. In an article on tax shelters published in a leading financial periodical, a tax shelter promoter admitted that "we don't even want people to buy our program based on (the program's) economics. . . . If we find that anybody's going to purchase a program from us based on the expectation or necessity of receiving money, we recommend he not try it. . . ." Also, careful examination of the tax shelter promotional literature shows that, typically, a substantial part of your initial cash contribution is used to pay promotional expenses rather than to purchase assets to be used in the tax shelter investment.

Strategy Tip

The reduction of the top bracket from 70 percent to 50 percent, effective January 1, 1982, makes it more important than ever to consider the risks of a proposed tax shelter deal and the soundness of the projected write-offs. The benefits of such tax shelters to you if you were in a tax bracket above 50 percent is now less with a 50 percent top bracket.

What are the tax shelter investments favored by the new law?

The tax shelter investments favored under the new law are real estate, particularly low-income housing and rehabilitation of old buildings; oil and gas; energy property; and perhaps research and experimentation. Here are the details.

Real Estate

The more rapid write-offs under ACRS that we have described in Chapter 9 will favor a variety of shelters that involve investments in property eligible for ACRS treatment. The principal winner is real estate. Under the new law, the cost of buildings can be recovered over a fifteen-year period. This is considerably shorter than the forty-sixty-year useful life rules applicable to buildings of substantial size under the prior law. The same is true, on a lesser scale, for other business assets that will now be recovered over shortened three-, five-, or ten-year periods. But since the most dramatic changes under ACRS call for more rapid tax write-offs for buildings (i.e., office buildings, hotels, factories, apartments, etc.), real estate will be a popular source of tax shelters under the new law. Also, the cut in the capital gains rate will permit you to retain a larger share of any profits if the real estate is sold.

Within the real estate area, low-income housing shelters should flourish.

The new law favors new construction of low-income housing projects by permanently exempting low-income housing from the construction period interest and taxes capitalization requirement applicable to other kinds of real estate shelters. The recapture rules are also more attractive since, as residential real estate, such property is not subject to full recapture of all ACRS claimed deductions, only those that exceed straight line. The new law has also increased the per-dwelling maximum investment (from $20,000 to $40,000) for shelters that rehabilitate low-income housing and write the rehabilitation costs off over five years.

Other rehabilitation investments should also do well under the new law. The 1981 law has provided for a sliding scale of tax credits for rehabilitation of buildings at least thirty years old. The credit is 15 percent for structures at least thirty years old; 20 percent for structures at least forty years old; and 25 percent for certified historic structures. The 15 percent and 20 percent credits are limited to nonresidential buildings. However, the 25 percent credit for historical rehabilitation is available for nonresidential and residential buildings.

Strategy Tip

If you are looking for new office space, consider rehabilitating an old building to get the special credit.

Oil and Gas

The new ACRS rules will probably not have much impact on oil and gas investors. If you have limited partnership interests in oil and gas, the tax laws already give you fast write-offs for intangible drilling expenses rather than requiring amortization over the life of the well. But while these fast write-offs in the past triggered the minimum tax on the resulting "tax preference," the 50 percent maximum tax rate on investment income in 1982 and later years means that the fast write-offs won't cause your other investment income to be taxed at more than 50 percent. Finally, the modest windfall profit tax reductions are not expected to have much effect on oil and gas investments. However, if natural gas is decontrolled, look for these shelters to multiply.

Energy Projects

The investment credit at-risk rules that we have described in Chapter 11 do not apply to certain amounts borrowed on a nonrecourse basis for certain qualified energy property. This exception gives an advantage to tax shelters involving investments in this type of property. Qualified energy property includes solar or wind property, recycling equipment, hydroelectric generating property, biomass property, certain geothermal and ocean thermal equipment, and property comprising a system for using the same energy source for generating electric power or mechanical shaft power in combination with steam heat or other forms of energy.

In order to qualify for this exception from the at-risk rules (which applies as long as the energy tax credit is in effect), the investor must have an at-risk investment equal to at least 25 percent of the cost of the property. Also, any nonrecourse financing for the property must be made in the form of a level payment loan that is repaid in substantially equal installments, including both principal and interest. However, if the investor fails to make the required payments on the loan, some of the credit will be recaptured.

Research and Experimentation

The new credit for research and experimentation suggests that there will be limited partnerships that will finance corporate research and experimentation, take a share in any royalties on a new product, and promise to pass the new credit on to their partners. But it is not at all clear that the credit is available to a limited partnership that is merely organized to finance research and experimentation. The congressional committee reports state that the credit is available only for costs paid "in carrying on a trade or business" and that parties to "a financing arrangement" will not be eligible for the credit. However, if a limited partnership is engaged in some independent business of its own, it may be possible for it to qualify for the credit by financing research in a field that is not within its line of business.

Strategy Tip

Look very carefully at tax shelters that promise to pass through the research credit to the investors. The IRS is expected to issue regulations that will allow the credit in the case of research joint ventures by taxpayers who are otherwise engaged "in carrying on a trade or business" and who are entitled to the research results. You might consider holding off on investing in a research tax shelter until the IRS clarifies the law. Financing for the property must be repaid in substantially equal installments of both principal and interest. If the shelter can meet these requirements, the availability of the investment credit for investments involving nonrecourse borrowing provides an edge for energy property shelters over investments involving other forms of personal property. One final note: the cut in the maximum rates on investment income from 70 percent to 50 percent as of January 1, 1982, creates an added windfall to holders of old tax shelters. If you have been claiming deductions against income that would have been taxed at 70 percent, any future requirement that you restore those deductions to income will be subject to the 50 percent rate. The rate cut therefore provides an additional benefit to high-bracket taxpayers presently holding interests in shelters.

What are the tax shelter investments to avoid under the new law?

Commodity Straddles

As we later explain in Chapter 12, the new law cuts back on the use of commodity straddles through a number of restrictive provisions. Generally, the new law requires that gain and loss from regulated commodities future contracts must be reported on an annual basis. Therefore, unrealized gains and unrealized losses must be taken into account at year end for tax purposes. As a result, it is no longer possible to take offsetting positions so as to take losses (to offset other income) but defer realizing gains.

Shelters Involving Nonrecourse Financing of Property

As we explained in Chapter 11, the investment credit is now only available for investments in property for which you are at risk. This new provision represents an extension of existing laws that limit the losses you can claim in a transaction involving equipment leasing, farming, oil and gas ventures, motion picture films, and other shelters (but not real estate) to the amount you have at risk in the venture. The new provision means that if you borrow to purchase property, you will forfeit the investment if

- You are protected against loss of your investment.
- You are not personally liable for repayment of the debt.
- The lender has an interest other than as a creditor (such as an interest in the income of the project).
- The lender is a related party to the borrower.

The introduction of this new at-risk rule will likely have an adverse impact on the benefits of formerly popular tax shelters in print and book plates, phonograph records, and other similar shelters. These investments, in the past, were typically leveraged with nonrecourse financing and relied heavily on the availability of the investment credit. Since these shelters will no longer be eligible for the investment credit, without recourse financing, they are less attractive under the new law.

Strategy Tip

Regard with caution any tax shelter involving investment in personal property that promises the investment credit. The key to the availability of the investment credit is the nature of the borrowing.

14
Tax Straddles

One of the more popular tax avoidance techniques used in recent years has been the "tax straddle." Most of the tax straddles have involved commodities futures contracts, like corn or soybeans. The trading has also occurred in hard commodities such as gold and silver, and even in U.S. Treasury bills. It has been estimated that the annual revenue loss from the tax straddle device has been close to $1.3 billion a year. The new law has attempted to close this loophole.

What exactly is a tax straddle?

The straddle is a complicated transaction in which an investor will simultaneously enter into two commodities futures contracts to buy and sell some commodity in the future. A commodity futures contract obligates you to either buy or sell a specific commodity for a specific price and at a particular future date. The contract is not an option to purchase but in fact requires the person entering into the contract to complete the transaction. The party to the contract who will receive delivery of the commodity in the future is, in market terms, called the person in the "long" position. Conversely, the person required to make delivery is in the "short" position.

In a tax straddle, a person simultaneously holds both long and short positions in different delivery months usually (but not always) in the same commodity. For example, a person could enter into contracts to be long in soybeans in March 1982 and short in soybeans in June 1982. Or the taxpayer could go long in soybeans and short in soybean meal. In some cases, commodities are used which are completely different but which tend to increase or decrease in value in the same economic pattern, for example, long gold and short silver.

144

The long and short positions that are taken in a straddle are called "legs" of the straddle.

Straddle trading, accomplished by simultaneously taking long and short positions in a commodity, will cancel out the risks involved in your futures dealings. If you simultaneously establish both long and short positions in the same commodity, in equal amounts, your position will be in balance. Whether the price goes up or down, in one contract, you will have a gain, and in the other you will have a loss. Your risk in a straddle transaction is only the spread between the prices in the contract months, not the general fluctuation in the commodities price.

The basic benefit that taxpayers have sought to achieve through commodities tax straddles has been to defer or postpone into future tax years, a gain in the current year from an independent source. When such a deferral or postponement can be accomplished, you can temporarily retain the use of your tax money that would otherwise be due to the IRS on the gain transaction.

There are more complicated straddle transactions that have been used as tax avoidance techniques. One of these transactions was the so-called butterfly straddle. The butterfly straddle involved buying off-setting straddle positions. The taxpayer would buy four contracts rather than two. But the end result was the same: an attempt to postpone the tax from the current year into a future year by selling the loss leg of the straddle without incurring any economic risk because of the balance created by having a gain leg.

How does the new law close this loophole?

Regulated futures contracts

The accounting system used by the U.S. commodity exchanges requires that each day every outstanding contract that has unrealized paper gain or loss be credited or debited. This is done by the brokers who buy and sell the commodities contracts for their customers. Paper gains may be withdrawn, but paper losses must be covered before the next business day. These types of contracts are called "regulated future contracts."

The new law requires that gains or losses attributable to regulated futures contracts that are still open at year end will be treated as if the contracts had been sold on that day. The resulting paper gain or loss for the year is then treated as if 40 percent of it were short-term capital gain or capital loss and 60 percent of it were long-term capital gain or capital loss.

Hedging transactions

In many cases, futures contracts are not entered into as a tax shelter but for bona fide business reasons, as a legitimate hedge against market fluctuations in a needed commodity. For example, a cereal manufacturer may engage in trading in wheat and corn futures to ensure a supply of raw materials for its business. Under the new law, hedgers are given the opportunity to show clearly the nature of their transaction on their books on the day their contracts are purchased. Subsequently, all hedging gains and losses will be taxed to them as ordinary income.

You should note that the exemption for hedging transactions does not apply to syndicate transactions. The law defines a syndicate as a partnership or other entity in which more than 35 percent of the losses of the entity is allocable to limited partners or parties with limited liability in their business.

How does the new law treat commodities transactions that are not regulated futures contracts?

In the case of straddles involving transactions other than regulated futures contracts, the new law allows straddle losses only to the extent the losses exceed the unrealized gains on offsetting positions. Such offsetting positions must have been acquired before the loss transaction is consummated and must not be part of another straddle as of the end of the year.

What about interest and carrying charges?

The new law prohibits the current deduction of interest and carrying charges related to a position in a commodity unless they are matched by current income produced by the position. The excess of interest and other carrying charges over interest income must be capitalized. This rule applies to property acquired and positions established after June 23, 1981. However, it does not apply to hedging transactions.

How does the new law treat trading in government bonds?

Under prior law, government bonds or Treasury bills issued at a discount were a popular tax shelter because the IRS had ruled that the bonds themselves were not capital assets while futures contracts in the bonds were capital assets. Hence, it was possible for traders to claim ordinary losses on the bonds and capital gains on the futures contracts.

The new law provides that government bonds will now be treated as capital assets in determining gain or loss if they are issued at a discount and payable without interest in less than one year. Also, any gain on the sale of a short-term government bond is taxed as ordinary income to the extent it is attributable to the acquisition discount. Gains exceeding the acquisition discount are taxed as short-term capital gains.

How does the new law treat canceled positions in futures contracts?

Under prior law, traders would often cancel contracts to purchase or deliver or securities. Since these cancellations did not involve sales or exchanges, they would report the resulting losses as ordinary losses.

The new law bars the use of this strategy. It provides that gains or losses arising from cancellation of contracts for commodities that would be capital assets in the hands of the trader will likewise be taxed as capital gains or losses.

How does the new law treat dealer-held securities?

Under the old law, a dealer in securities had thirty days in which to identify a security as either part of his inventory (thereby subject to ordinary income tax treatment) or as investment property (thereby subject to capital gain or loss). The thirty-day rule permitted dealers to wait and see how a security would perform and then classify appreciated securities as investment property (eligible for capital gains) and depreciated securities as inventory (eligible for ordinary losses).

The new law abolishes the availability of this strategy. Dealers must now identify securities held for investment no later than the close of business on the day of acquisition. This rule applies to property acquired after August 13, 1981.

Part Three

Miscellaneous Provisions

15
Technical and
Special Amendments

Windfall Profit Tax and Other Energy Provisions

Royalty owners credit and exemptions

During the Carter administration, Congress enacted the Windfall Profits Tax in order to impose an additional tax on some of the unusual profit that became available to oil companies because of the deregulation of the price of crude oil. Shortly after the Windfall Profits Tax was enacted in 1980, it was discovered that the law subjected individuals who owned royalty interests in oil to tax at the same rate as the large companies engaged in oil and gas production. Congress therefore allowed a $1,000 refundable tax credit for royalty owners to apply against their Windfall Profit Tax liability. The credit applied only to individuals, estates, and family farm corporations and was applicable only to 1980.

The new law makes the royalty owner credit available for 1981 and increases it from $1,000 to $2,500.

For 1982 and later years, the new law provides a limited exemption from the Windfall Profits Tax for specified amounts of royalty production. For 1982 through 1984, the exemption is two barrels per day. For 1985 and 1986, the exemption is increased to three barrels per day.

Producer exemption

Independent producers are now eligible for reduced Windfall Profit Tax rates of up to 1,000 barrels per day of certain types of oil. The reduced rate applicable to an independent producer is 30 percent.

Under the new law, the stripper oil production of

independent producers is completely exempt from the Windfall Profit Tax beginning in 1983. The new law also provides that stripper oil cannot qualify for this exemption if it is produced from a stripper well property that has been transferred on or after July 23, 1981, by a producer other than an independent producer.

Reduced tax rate on newly discovered oil

Under present law, newly discovered oil is taxed at a 30 percent rate on the difference between its removal price and a severance tax adjustment plus a base price of $16.55 adjusted for grade, quality, location, and inflation plus 2 percent.

The new law reduces the Windfall Profit Tax rate on newly discovered oil from 30 percent to 15 percent, over five years, in accordance with the schedule in Table 30.

Table 30
REDUCTION IN TAX ON NEWLY DISCOVERED OIL

Year	Rate (%)
1982	27.5
1983	25.0
1984	22.5
1985	20.0
1986 and thereafter	15.0

Exemption for qualified charities

Under the old law, oil production attributable to certain qualifying charitable interests is exempt from the Windfall Profit Tax. Surprisingly, a charity organized for the residential placement, care, or treatment of delinquent, dependent, orphaned, neglected, or handicapped children has not been qualified for this exemption. Now the new law extends the existing Windfall Profit Tax exemption to include these charities.

Production credit for certain gases

Present law allows a credit for the production of certain types of natural gas. Under the new law, producers may not claim the credit if they elect the incentive price for the gas under the Natural Gas Policy Act. The purpose of the new law is to prevent any producer from obtaining the benefits of the production credit and the incentive price.

Restricted Property

Under the old tax law, property transferred to an employee as compensation for services is taxable at the time the property is received by the employee as long as the property is not subject to a substantial risk of forfeiture or if the employee can freely transfer the property. Certain provisions of the securities law provide that the "short-swing" profits on the sale of company stock by company insiders, such as officers, directors, and so on, are subject to recovery by the company. Short-swing profits are gains taken within a short period of time, as prescribed by the securities law. As a result, company insiders have sought to postpone tax on the values of company stock they receive as compensation until the stock is no longer subject to the short-swing profit rules of the securities laws. The courts have rejected these attempts. They have ruled that the provisions of the securities law do not restrict transferability for purposes of the tax laws and that such short-swing stock is fully taxable on receipt.

The new law overturns these court decisions and upholds the taxpayer's position on this question. Under the new law, the provisions of the securities law are taken into account to postpone taxation until the short-swing profits rules no longer may apply. A similar rule applies to certain restrictions under the Securities Exchange Commission (SEC) accounting rules.

The new law is effective for tax years ending after December 31, 1981.

Strategy Tip

Companies planning to compensate top management with company stock should wait until next year if the short-swing profit rules of the SEC are applicable.

Fringe Benefits Regulations

During the Carter administration, the Treasury Department considered issuing special regulations on the income tax treatment of fringe benefits. These regulations would have presumably covered the tax status of courtesy discounts, free tuition for children of faculty, free limousine service for employees, free travel for airline personnel, and the like. These proposals promoted strong opposition, and prior to June 1, 1981, Congress prohibited the Treasury from issuing these regulations. The new law extends this prohibition until December 31, 1983. The delay presumably will give Congress time to study the area and write new laws.

State Legislators' Travel Expenses

Under the old law, state legislators could elect to treat their residences within their districts as their "tax home." As a result, they could deduct their costs for lodging and meals while in the state capital as business costs incurred while "away from home." If the legislator made the tax election, his allowable deduction was equal to the sum of his legislative days multiplied by the applicable per diem rate for federal employees in the state capital.

The new law extends and modifies this provision for all tax years beginning on or after January 1, 1976. Under the new provision, a state legislators who elect to do this will be considered to have spent (for business purposes) an amount equal to his or her legislative days multiplied by the greater of the federal employee per diem or the state employee per diem but not more than 110 percent of the federal per diem. This amount per day is deductible whether or not the legislator spends the night away from home. The new state legislator rule, however, does not apply to legislators who live within fifty miles of the state capitol building.

Campaign Funds

Under the prior law, candidates for election to Congress must designate one "principal campaign committee" to receive contributions and make expenditures on the candidate's behalf. A candidate's campaign organization was generally exempt from taxation. However, if the organization had income, such as interests earned on bank accounts, it was subject to the highest rate of the corporate income tax (46 percent) rather than at the graduated rate.

For tax years beginning after December 31, 1981, the new law applies the generally applicable graduated corporate income tax rates to such income.

Motor Carrier Operating Authorities

The old law did not permit a loss deduction for the decrease in *value* of a license or permit if the license or permit was not entirely worthless but continued to have value as a right to carry on a business.

Since the deregulation of motor carriers has substantially reduced the value of licenses, the new law permits an ordinary loss deduction for the decrease in their value even though the carriers are still conducting business under the licenses. The deduction can now be taken ratably over a sixty-month period and is limited to the taxpayer's cost of the license. This new provision applies to tax years ending after June 30, 1980.

Adjustments to Bad Debt Deductions for Commercial Banks

The new law provides an adjustment in how commercial banks compute their deduction for bad debts. The adjustment only applies to taxable years beginning in 1982. It provides that a bank can increase its reserve for bad debts in the amount of 1.0 percent of its outstanding eligible loans. Under the old law, the applicable percentage was 0.6 percent. On a one-time basis, the new law therefore provides for a more liberal bad-debt allowance for the year 1982.

Reorganizations Involving Financially Troubled Thrift Institutions

The new law relaxes the requirements for tax-free mergers of financially troubled thrift institutions. The amendment applies only after certification of need by either the federal home loan bank board, the federal savings and loan insurance corporation, or an equivalent state authority.

Tax Treatment of Mutual Savings Banks that Convert to Stock Associations

The new law makes two changes that are designed to facilitate the conversion of mutual savings banks into stock associations. First, the law provides that a stock association that is subject to the same regulation as a mutual savings bank is to be treated as a mutual savings bank and therefore eligible to compute its deductions for bad debts under the same rules as a mutual savings bank. Second, the new law grants mutual savings banks special tax treatment on their life insurance business. The new law also clarifies that amounts paid to depositors of such stock associations are deductible to the same extent as amounts paid to depositors of mutual savings banks.

These changes are effective with respect to tax

years ending after the date of the new law's enactment, August 13, 1981.

Tax-Exempt Bonds for Purchase of Mass Transit Equipment

A state or local government may issue tax-exempt bonds to finance the construction of public facilities, including "mass commuting facilities." However, "mass commuting facilities" has never included the equipment used for commuting purposes such as buses, subway cars, or railroad passenger cars used in the commuting system. The new law now permits a state or local government to issue tax-exempt bonds for qualified mass commuting vehicles leased to a mass transit system that is wholly owned by the government. The law requires that bonds for this purpose must be issued after August 13, 1981, and before January 1, 1985.

Tax-Exempt Bonds for Volunteer Fire Departments

Generally, tax-exempt municipal bonds must be issued by a state or political subdivision of the state. The new law now permits volunteer fire departments to issue tax-exempt obligations if they are an organization (1) that is organized and operated to provide fire fighting or emergency medical services in an area that is not provided with any other fire-fighting services and (2) that is required, by written agreement, to furnish such services.

This change will apply to bonds issued after December 31, 1980. However, Congress made the provision retroactive with respect to certain bonds held by the First Bank and Trust Company of Indianapolis, Indiana, which were issued during 1980.

Private Foundations

The new law reduces the amount of income that tax-exempt private foundations must distribute without triggering a tax. In the past, private foundations had to distribute to their beneficiaries income in excess of their "minimum investment return" (generally 5 percent). The new law abolishes that requirement by lowering their required pay-out to their minimum investment return.

Railroad Retirement Tax Act Changes

The new law makes two tax rate changes with respect to the railroad retirement tax on compensation paid for services after September 30, 1981. First, an additional 2 percent tax is imposed on the earnings of railway employees. Second, the excise tax on railroad employers is increased from 9.5 percent of taxable compensation to 11.75 percent. These taxes may not be imposed on wages in excess of $2,475 per month. The new law makes certain changes in the timing of the "compensation" of railway employees.

Unemployment Tax Status for Certain Fishing Boat Services

Certain crew members of fishing boats are treated as self-employed individuals rather than employees and therefore are not subject to the Social Security tax and income tax withholding. However, even though they are not subject to Social Security taxes and withholding, these fishermen are subject to Federal Employment Tax Act (FUTA) (unemployment) taxes if their services are related to catching halibut or salmon for commercial purposes or if they work on a vessel of ten net tons.

The new law provides that, during 1981, wages paid to fishing boat crew members who are self-employed for purposes of Social Security taxes and income tax withholdings will not be subject to FUTA taxes.

Two-Year Extension of Telephone Excise Tax at 1 Percent

The excise tax imposed on communication services (local telephone, toll telephone, and teletype writer services) for 1981 is 2 percent of the amount paid for such services. The tax was scheduled to be 1 percent for 1982 and to expire as of January 1, 1983.

Under the new law, the telephone excise tax will be extended at 1 percent for two more years (1983 and 1984) and will now expire on January 1, 1985.

Confidentiality of Certain IRS Information

Under the prior law, provisions that restricted the disclosure of tax returns and return information did not make clear whether the IRS legally could refuse to disclose information that is used to develop standards for auditing tax returns. Many lawsuits were brought under the Freedom of Information Act seeking disclosure of this information. But the IRS resisted these requests in the courts even though some of the decisions in court did not go the government's way.

Now Congress has come to the IRS's rescue. The new law provides that the IRS can refuse to disclose this information if the commissioner of the IRS determines that disclosure will seriously impair assessment, collection, or enforcement under the IRS laws. On August 14, 1981, the commissioner of the IRS made such a determination. It is therefore expected that this kind of information will not be disclosed. The new law applies retroactively to July 19, 1981.

Modification of Foreign Investment Company Provisions

Under the old law, the gain on the sale or exchange of stock in a foreign investment company is taxed as ordinary income to the extent it is attributable to earnings derived after 1962. Once a foreign corporation becomes a foreign investment company, the ordinary income treatment applies even to earnings derived before the foreign corporation became a foreign investment company.

Under the new law, your gain on the sale of stock in

a foreign investment company attributable to earnings and profits derived before the foreign corporation became a foreign investment company will not be automatically subject to ordinary income tax treatment. However, gain on the sale of the stock of foreign corporations that are 50 percent owned by U.S. shareholders and are engaged primarily in the business of investing and reinvesting in or trading in securities continues to be subject to ordinary income tax (to the extent of corporate earnings) where such sales are made by persons owning 10 percent or more of the corporation's stock.

The new law is effective for sales and exchanges after August 13, 1981.

Foreign Investment in U.S. Real Estate

Under present law, foreign persons selling U.S. real estate after June 18, 1980, are subject to U.S. taxation on that sale. Foreign persons selling stock in a U.S. corporation having 50 percent or more of its gross asset value in U.S. real estate interests are subject to taxation. Finally, the distributions of U.S. real estate interests by a foreign corporation are generally subject to tax. The taxation of sales of U.S. real estate interests apply to transactions covered by an international tax treaty, but, in general, not until January 1, 1985, if such tax treatment would be contrary to the applicable treaty.

The new law makes certain changes in the tax treatment of foreign investment in U.S. real estate. These are as follows:

Virgin Islands corporations

A U.S. real estate interest includes an interest in real property located in the United States or the Virgin Islands. Double taxation by both the United States and the government of the Virgin Islands is prevented by providing that a person subject to tax files the necessary returns only with the particular country (the United States or the Virgin Islands) in which the property is located. The sale of an interest in real estate located in the Virgin Islands is considered to be foreign-source income to U.S. taxpayers.

Partnership assets

For purposes of determining whether a corporation is a U.S. real estate holding corporation, a corporate partner takes into account its proportionate share of all assets (not only U.S. real estate interests) of the partnership. The same rules apply to trusts and estates in which a corporation has an interest.

Treasury authority

The new law makes clear that the Treasury has the authority to establish rules for the recognition and nonrecognition of gain by a foreign corporation in certain transactions entered into for purposes of avoiding U.S. income tax.

Nondiscrimination

The new law provides that under certain conditions any foreign corporation may elect to be treated as a U.S. corporation for purposes of determining whether its activities constitute engaging in a trade or business within the United States. The election is available if the foreign corporation owns an interest in U.S. real estate; the corporation is entitled to nondiscriminatory treatment with respect to its real estate interests under a tax treaty.

Indirect holdings

For purposes of determining whether a foreign corporation has substantial U.S. real estate investors, a foreign corporation must look through to the assets of any U.S. corporation in which the foreign corporation has an interest.

Contributions to capital

The new law specifically makes clear that a nonresident alien individual or a foreign corporation will recognize gain on the transfer of an interest in U.S. real estate to a foreign corporation if the transfer is paid in the surplus or is made as a contribution to capital of the foreign corporation.

Liquidation of foreign corporations

Foreign corporations that were acquired during the period that began after December 31, 1979, and before November 26, 1980, may choose to be treated as a U.S. corporation for certain liquidation treatment rules. For all other purposes, the foreign corporation will be treated as a foreign corporation.

The new law also relieves the double tax burden that would otherwise apply to a U.S. person who purchases the stock of a foreign corporation that holds U.S. real estate. It does this by giving those shareholders who acquire their interest between December 31, 1979, and November 26, 1980, to the effective date of the Foreign Investment in Real Property Tax Act, a credit against any tax imposed on them on the surrender of their stock in the liquidating foreign corporation. The credit is equal to the tax imposed on the liquidating foreign corporation on the sale of the U.S. real estate. The rule applies only if the U.S. person continuously held the stock since June 18, 1980, the effective date of the foreign investment in U.S. real estate legislation.

Appendix A

INCOME TAX RATES
SINGLE INDIVIDUALS

If taxable income exceeds this base amount	But does not exceed this amount	1981*		1982		1983		1984 and after	
		You pay this amount	PLUS this % of the excess over the base amount	You pay this amount	PLUS this % of the excess over the base amount	You pay this amount	PLUS this % of the excess over the base amount	You pay this amount	PLUS this % of the excess over the base amount
0	2,300	0		0		0		0	
2,300	3,400	0	14	0	12	0	11	0	11
3,400	4,400	154	16	132	14	121	13	121	12
4,400	6,500	314	18	272	16	251	15	241	14
6,500	8,500	692	19	608	17	566	15	535	15
8,500	10,800	1,072	21	948	19	866	17	835	16
10,800	12,900	1,555	24	1,385	22	1,257	19	1,203	18
12,900	15,000	2,059	26	1,847	23	1,656	21	1,581	20
15,000	18,200	2,605	30	2,330	27	2,097	24	2,001	23
18,200	23,500	3,565	34	3,194	31	2,965	28	2,737	26
23,500	28,800	5,367	39	4,837	35	4,349	32	4,115	30
28,800	34,100	7,434	44	6,692	40	6,045	36	5,705	34
34,100	41,500	9,766	49	8,812	44	7,953	40	7,507	38
41,500	55,300	13,392	55	12,068	50	10,913	45	10,319	42
55,300	81,800	20,982	63			17,123	50	16,115	48
81,800	108,300	37,677	68					28,835	50
108,300		55,697	70						

*For 1981, multiply the resulting figure by 0.9875 to take into account the 1.25% tax cut effective October 1, 1981.

162

INCOME TAX RATES

MARRIED INDIVIDUALS FILING JOINT RETURNS AND SURVIVING SPOUSES

If taxable income exceeds this base amount	But does not exceed this amount	1981* You pay this amount	1981* PLUS this % of the excess over the base amount	1982 You pay this amount	1982 PLUS this % of the excess over the base amount	1983 You pay this amount	1983 PLUS this % of the excess over the base amount	1984 and after You pay this amount	1984 and after PLUS this % of the excess over the base amount
0	3,400	0	14	0	12	0	11	0	11
3,400	5,400	0	16	0	14	0	13	0	12
5,500	7,600	294	18	252	16	231	15	231	14
7,600	11,900	630	21	546	19	504	17	483	16
11,900	16,000	1,404	24	1,234	22	1,149	19	1,085	18
16,000	20,200	2,265	28	2,013	25	1,846	23	1,741	22
20,200	24,600	3,273	32	2,937	29	2,644	26	2,497	25
24,600	29,900	4,505	37	4,037	33	3,656	30	3,465	28
29,900	35,200	6,201	43	5,574	39	5,034	35	4,790	33
35,200	45,800	8,162	49	7,323	44	6,624	40	6,274	38
45,800	60,000	12,720	54	11,457	49	10,334	44	9,772	42
60,000	85,600	19,678	59	17,705	50	16,014	48	15,168	45
85,600	109,400	33,502	64	30,249		27,278	50	25,920	49
109,400	162,400	47,544	68			38,702		36,630	50
162,400	215,400	81,464	70					62,600	
215,400		117,504							

*For 1981, multiply the resulting figure by 0.9875 to take into account the 1.25% tax cut effective October 1, 1981.

163

INCOME TAX RATES
MARRIED INDIVIDUALS FILING SEPARATE RETURNS

If taxable income exceeds this base amount	But does not exceed this amount	1981*		1982		1983		1984 and after	
		You pay this amount	PLUS this % of the excess over the base amount	You pay this amount	PLUS this % of the excess over the base amount	You pay this amount	PLUS this % of the excess over the base amount	You pay this amount	PLUS this % of the excess over the base amount
0	1,700	0		0		0		0	
1,700	2,750	0	14	0	12	0	11	0	11
2,750	3,800	147	16	126	14	115	13	115	12
3,800	5,950	315	18	273	16	252	15	241	14
5,950	8,000	702	21	617	19	574	17	542	16
8,000	10,100	1,132.50	24	1,006	22	923	19	870	18
10,100	12,300	1,636.50	28	1,468	25	1,322	23	1,248	22
12,300	14,950	2,252.50	32	2,018	29	1,828	26	1,732	25
14,950	17,600	3,100.50	37	2,787	33	2,517	30	2,395	28
17,600	22,900	4,081	43	3,661	39	3,312	35	3,137	33
22,900	30,000	6,360	49	5,728	44	5,167	40	4,886	38
30,000	42,800	9,839	54	8,852	49	8,007	44	7,584	42
42,800	54,700	16,751	59	15,124	50	13,639	48	12,960	45
54,700	81,200	23,772	64			19,351	50	18,315	49
81,200	107,700	40,732	68					31,300	50
107,700		58,752	70						

*For 1981, multiply the resulting figure by 0.9875 to take into account the 1.25% tax cut effective October 1, 1981.

164

INCOME TAX RATES
HEADS OF HOUSEHOLDS

If taxable income exceeds this base amount	But does not exceed this amount	1981* You pay this amount	1981* PLUS this % of the excess over the base amount	1982 You pay this amount	1982 PLUS this % of the excess over the base amount	1983 You pay this amount	1983 PLUS this % of the excess over the base amount	1984 and after You pay this amount	1984 and after PLUS this % of the excess over the base amount
0	2,300	0		0		0		0	
2,300	4,400	0	14	0	12	0	11	0	11
4,400	6,500	294	16	252	14	231	11	231	12
6,500	8,700	630	18	546	16	504	15	483	14
8,700	11,800	1,026	22	898	20	834	18	791	17
11,800	15,000	1,708	24	1,518	22	1,392	19	1,318	18
15,000	18,000	2,474	26	2,222	23	2,000	21	1,894	20
18,000	23,500	3,308	31	2,958	28	2,672	25	2,534	24
23,500	28,800	4,951	36	4,442	32	3,997	29	3,806	28
28,800	34,100	6,859	42	6,138	38	5,534	34	5,290	32
34,100	44,700	9,085	46	8,152	41	7,336	37	6,986	35
44,700	60,600	13,961	54	12,498	49	11,258	44	10,696	42
60,600	81,800	22,547	59	20,289	50	18,254	48	17,374	45
81,800	108,300	35,055	63			28,430	50	26,914	48
108,300	161,300	51,750	68					39,632	50
161,300		87,790	70						

*For 1981, multiply the resulting figure by 0.9875 to take into account the 1.25% tax cut effective October 1, 1981.

Appendix B
WHEN THE MAJOR CHANGES TAKE EFFECT

Provision	Effective Date
Accelerated Cost Recovery System	Property placed in service after December 31, 1980
Accumulated Earnings Tax Credit Increase	Taxable years beginning after December 31, 1981
Adoption Expenses	Taxable years beginning after December 31, 1980
All-Saver Certificates	Issued after October 30, 1981 and before January 1, 1983
Capital Gains for Individuals 20% Maximum Tax	June 9, 1981
Charitable Contributions by corporations of Scientific Research Property	Contributions after August 13, 1981
Charitable Deductions for Non-Itemizers	January 1, 1982 to December 31, 1986
Child and Dependent Care Credit Increase	January 1, 1982
Confidentiality of Certain IRS Information	Disclosures after July 19, 1981
Corporate Charitable Contributions—Increase in Limitation	January 1, 1982
Corporate Rate Cuts	January 1, 1982
Expensing Privilege for Certain ACRS Assets	Assets placed in service after December 31, 1981
Employee Gifts and Awards	Taxable years ending on or after August 13, 1981
Employee Stock Ownership Plan	Taxable years beginning after December 31, 1982
Estate and Gift Tax Changes	
Annual Gift Tax Exclusion	Transfers made after December 31, 1981
Annual Payment of Gift Tax	Transfers made after December 31, 1981
Charitable Gifts of Copyrightable Works	Transfers made after December 31, 1981
Disclaimers of Property	Transfers creating an interest after January 1, 1982
Generation Skipping Transfers	Effective date postponed until January 1, 1983
Installment Payment of Estate Taxes	January 1, 1982
Jointly Held Property	Estates of decedents dying after December 31, 1981
Orphan's Deduction	Estates of decedents dying after December 31, 1981
Rate Cuts	Gifts made after and estates of decedents dying after December 31, 1981
Special Use Valuation	Estate of decedents dying after December 31, 1981
Transfers Made Within Three Years—of Death	Estates of decedents dying after December 31, 1981
Unified Credit Increase	Gifts made after and estates of decedents dying after December 31, 1981
Unlimited Gift Tax Exclusion for Education and Health Care Payments	Transfers made after December 31, 1981
Estimated Tax Declarations, threshold amount increase	Taxable years beginning after December 31, 1981
Estimated Tax Payments by large corporations	Taxable years beginning after December 31, 1981
Foreign Earned Income Exclusion	January 1, 1982
Foreign Investment Company Provisions	Sales or exchanges after August 13, 1981 in taxable years ending after that date
Foreign Investment in U.S. Real Property	Dispositions after June 18, 1980 in taxable years ending after that date
Fringe Benefits Regulation	Ban extended through December 31, 1983
Futures Contract Marked to Market	Property acquired and positions established after June 23, 1981 in taxable years ending after that date

Provision	Effective Date
Group Legal Services Plans	Extended through December 31, 1984
Indexing	Taxable years beginning after December 31, 1984
Individual Income Tax Rate Cuts	5% reduction October 1, 1981; 10% reduction July 1, 1982; 10% reduction July 2, 1983
Individual Retirement Accounts	Taxable years beginning after December 31, 1981
Interest, Exclusion for Net Interest	Taxable years beginning after December 31, 1984
Interest Rate on Underpayments Overpayments	Adjustments effective February 1, 1982
Inventory Rules	Taxable years beginning after December 31, 1981
Investment Tax Credit	
ACRS property	Property placed in service after December 31, 1980
Rehabilitated property	Expenditures after December 31, 1981
Used Property	Property placed in service after December 31, 1980
Keogh Plan changes	Taxable years beginning after December 31, 1981
Low-Income Housing	Expenditures after December 31, 1980
Exemption from amortizing certain construction period interest and taxes	Exemption made permanent
Increase in per unit expenditure limit	Taxable years beginning after December 31, 1980
Marriage Tax Penalty Relief	January 1, 1982
Maximum Tax	January 1, 1982
Minimum Tax	Property placed in service after December 31, 1980 in taxable years beginning after that date
Penalties	
False withholding information	Acts and failures to act after December 31, 1981
Information Return Requirements	Returns and statements required to be furnished after December 31, 1981
Negligence	Taxes paid after December 31, 1981
Valuation overstatement	Returns filed after December 31, 1981
Private Foundations, Payout Requirements	Taxable years beginning after December 31, 1981
Public Utility Stock Dividend Reinvestment	Distributions after December 31, 1981 but before January 1, 1986
Railroad Retirement Taxes tax rate increase	Compensation paid after September 30, 1981
Recapture on Disposition of ACRS Property	Property placed in service after December 31, 1980 in taxable years ending after such date
Research and Experimentation Credit	Amounts paid or incurred after June 30, 1981, and before January 1, 1986
Residences, personal, $125,000 exclusion of gain on sale	Residences sold or exchanged after July 20, 1981
Residences, personal, 2 year rollover period	Residences sold or exchanged after July 20, 1981, or on or before July 20, 1981 if the former 18 month rollover period expires on or after July 20, 1981
Restricted Property	Taxable years ending after December 31, 1981
Royalty Owners Credit and Exemption	After December 31, 1981
Simplified Employee Pension Plans	Taxable years beginning after December 31, 1981
State Legislators Travel Expenses	Taxable years beginning on or after January 1, 1976
Stock Options, Incentive	Options granted on or after January 1, 1976 and exercised on or after January 1, 1981 or outstanding on that date
Subchapter S Corporations	Taxable years beginning after December 31, 1981

Provision	Effective Date
Withholding Tax	
Rate reductions	5% reduction, October 1, 1981
	10% reduction, July 1, 1982
	10% reduction, July 1, 1983
Penalty for overstated deposits claims	Returns filed after August 13, 1981

Index

ABOUT THE AUTHORS

STUART A. SMITH is a Washington tax lawyer. During the past 17 years, he has practiced both with the government and in the private sector. Mr. Smith has argued numerous tax cases before the United States Supreme Court and the Federal Courts of Appeals. He has taught tax courses at the Georgetown University Law Center, has participated in the New York University Tax Institute, and has contributed articles to several professional tax journals. Mr. Smith lives in Washington, D.C.

JANET R. SPRAGENS is a tax professor on the faculty of the American University Law School in Washington, D.C. Over the past 12 years, in addition to her teaching, she has practiced tax law both with the government and in private practice. Ms. Spragens is the author of several scholarly articles that have been published in tax journals. She also wrote a weekly column on law for the *Washington Star* and the *Detroit News* for several years. Ms. Spragens is a graduate of Wellsley College and the George Washington University Law School. She currently lives in Washington, D.C. with her two children.